BOARDROOM
SELLING

BOARDROOM SELLING

PROVEN STRATEGIES FOR
SELLING TO DECISION MAKERS

BOB HECKMAN

BROWN BOOKS PUBLISHING GROUP
DALLAS, TEXAS

BOARDROOM SELLING: PROVEN STRATEGIES FOR
SELLING TO DECISION MAKERS

Manufactured in the United States of America.

For information, please contact:
Brown Books Publishing Group
16200 North Dallas Parkway, Suite 170
Dallas, Texas 75248
www.brownbooks.com
972-381-0009

ISBN 0-9744597-8-X
LCCN 2004112574
2 3 4 5 6 7 8 9 10

CONTENTS

ACKNOWLEDGMENTS

Writing a book is hard! The magazine articles were much easier; a book, however, is a daunting effort. Many sheets of paper have been filed away in some forgotten drawer (or torn up) in attempts to capture several decades of sales experience. Finally it has all come together in *Boardroom Selling*. The staff at Brown Books Publishing Group has been very helpful in making the process go smoother.

Encouragement from friends, clients, and family provided the spark needed when my engine seemed out of gas. A very special thanks to my bride of many years, Sandy, for her willingness to listen, offer suggestions, and provide constant positive support!

INTRODUCTION

It's December 31.

I'm down to two prospects. To make my quota for the year, I have to sell one of them before midnight. As you might imagine, I'm totally focused, prepared, motivated, and enthusiastic. I'm ready to do whatever it takes to close those deals. I'm at my very best . . . I am a sales machine!

If you've been in sales for any length of time, you can identify with my situation.

So, here is my question.

If we can perform at this accelerated level on December 31, what happens on the other selling days of the year? Are we as prepared and focused? Why don't we perform at this level every day of the year?

Walking the Talk . . .

If you were about to take a class on home remodeling, you'd want to be sure your instructors have plenty of experience. Not just talked about it, or studied the subject, but actually did the work. Wouldn't you want to know if they've measured lumber, pounded nails, and painted trim? It's a fair question to ask of anyone who is going to teach you how to stain cabinets . . . or how to close a sale.

I've spent four decades selling, managing salespeople, and teaching others how to sell. I teach and write on the subject of selling, but first and foremost, I've made my living through direct sales. In fact, I still do. Now I want to share my experiences with you in the hope that they will help you sell even more effectively. How much more effectively depends on your willingness to adopt and implement the boardroom selling strategies presented in this book.

What This Book Is, and What It Isn't

My purpose in writing this book is not to create a start-to-finish instructional guide on the sales process. Others have done that job well enough. My goal is to show you how the world's best salespeople supercharge their efforts by focusing on their best customers and solid prospects . . . with a minimum of cold calling!

It's every sales professional's ambition to "sell in the boardroom." That's where the action is; it's where the big decisions are made. That's where we want to be! Just imagine presenting our services to the key leaders of the organization . . .

However, the reality is this: Very few sales professionals get to present to the board of directors of any organization! Your presentation may be delivered in some form to the board, but almost always a very senior member of the management team handles the assignment.

Should this throw cold water on the goal of boardroom selling? Absolutely not! The preparation you would put into a boardroom presentation — if you were fortunate enough to get that audience — is vital. Therefore, it's vital at any level. Let me suggest that an insurance agent talking to a young couple about their first insurance policy is in "the boardroom." The boardroom in this case may be at the kitchen table, but the preparation, delivery, and interaction are just as significant to both the young couple and the insurance agent.

When you brief your prospect or customer on a new product or service prior to that person taking it to the next level for approval, you are selling at the boardroom level. It just happens that someone else may actually deliver your presentation.

Here's what you'll learn in this book:

◆ The logic of UniqueConnect Selling
◆ Intent, Information, and Insight: A salesperson's most valuable assets
◆ How to use a proven Sales Tool Kit gained through years of selling

Is selling an art or a science? Probably a bit of both. In my view, selling requires the ability to discover and fully understand your client's needs, challenges, and opportunities. It is then understanding how your solutions and products match or map to those needs. The result should be a well-constructed business case for an action plan and considerable value for your client.

If you believe in constantly improving your knowledge and refining your selling skills, this book is meant for you. Here's some good news: You don't have to have the gift of gab or be glib and "fast on your feet" to sell. The principles outlined in this book assume you have a *genuine interest* in the success of your customer or prospect. If you do, you will find personal success as a result.

Let's get started.

Chapter 1

A TAP ON MY WINDOW

We all need a little help now and then.

I got exactly that on my very first day in sales. Newly hired by IBM, I had just completed the legendary sales-training courses in White Plains, New York, and had been assigned my sales territory. I was given a copy of the sales commission plan and a user's list of the IBM customers in my territory. Straightening my tie and clutching my sales literature, I jumped in the car and was off to make the very first sales call of my professional life. It was 8:30 on a Monday morning and I was terrified!

It occurred to me that it might be a good idea to drive around a bit and to locate my customers' offices on my map. You know, get a "lay of the land." So I scouted my new territory until mid-morning. Because it was a cold February day in Cleveland, Ohio, I picked up a cup of coffee, then sat in my car. I reviewed my map and my user's list and started writing down names on my call pad. Just two weeks earlier, in the sales training class, I was told that selling would be easier. Everything seemed to work there! I wondered if everyone went through this sinking feeling.

A couple of minutes later, a tap on my window startled me. Dan Kramer, a respected senior IBM salesman in our office, motioned for me to lower my window.

"You know you're sitting in the middle of what used to be part of my territory," Dan said.

"Yes," I said. "I was just getting ready to make a couple of calls."

"But you haven't made any yet, have you?"

"No," I replied.

Then Dan said with a smile, "Would you like to meet some customers?"

"I sure would."

So over the next couple of hours, he introduced me to four or five of his former customers and got me started on what has been a long and rewarding career in sales. To this day, I sometimes think if I hadn't heard Dan's tap on my window, I might still be sitting in the car, looking at my map, and drinking a cold cup of coffee!

Dan showed me what it meant to be a true professional. He got me going on that first, tough day in the field. He also created the basis for this book—calling on current customers and carefully-identified prospects beats cold calling any day.

Lessons Learned

I didn't realize it that cold Ohio morning, but Dan Kramer had taught me two career-changing lessons.

One
Cold calls are tough.

Two
You can dramatically increase your business by focusing your sales efforts almost exclusively on your current customers and well-qualified prospects.

That's what this book is about. Successful salespeople have learned to concentrate on developing their present customers. They've also learned how to identify good prospects without blindly knocking on every door. Can you be successful making tons of cold calls? Yes, but there's a much better way.

If you aspire to sell smarter and sell more, read on.

WE CALL THEM COLD FOR A REASON

Sure, even the best salesperson will make cold calls now and then. I do so myself when I have a few spare minutes or if an unexpected opportunity arises.

Some sales pros may claim they enjoy making cold calls, but I think those claims are mostly macho bluster. As anyone who has ever done it will tell you, cold calling is a time–consuming and punishing endeavor. It does not produce the results you get from a more focused and well-thought-out selling strategy.

Remember, cold calls are not a lot of fun for the folks on the other side of the desk either. Cold calls can be an imposition and a distraction for the prospect. As a matter of fact, I don't enjoy getting cold calls from salespeople I don't know, and I suspect you don't either. Time is precious to all of us, and responding to cold calls has a low priority.

So if *we* don't like them when we're on the receiving end, you can bet your customers and prospects don't either.

A BETTER WAY TO SELL

After that first day of calls with Dan, I spent several weeks banging my head against the wall, making cold calls, and trying to pull new business out of thin air. It was frustrating and demoralizing. Worse, it did not yield anything close to acceptable sales results.

Some of my cold calls did result in possible business, but the percentage was low . . . probably less than 15 percent. What a career! I face rejection 85 percent of the time and then get to do it all over again the next day!

Then it hit me.

What I enjoyed most when Dan and I made calls was talking to customers. They were friendly and shared information. They also seemed glad to see us. And they were mine!

I realized that my IBM user's list was my ticket to sales success. Think about it. Customers who had purchased in the past may buy again in the future. What a novel idea! There might be others in their company who would buy. These same customers might even know people in other companies who may need my products or services. Wow! I had discovered a treasure map lying right there on the front seat next to me.

Over time, that IBM user's list led me to some of the hottest prospects I would ever find. The balance between cold calls and planned customer visits shifted dramatically, and so did my success.

CUSTOMERS FIRST

That day marked the beginning of a new way of doing things. I quickly became a disciple of what might be called the customer-focused school of sales.

I spent the next six months of my career visiting and revisiting the companies on my user's list. I asked questions, but most important, I listened. I learned about their business, their requirements, and their personalities. I researched what they had purchased, what had worked, and what had not. I dedicated myself to doing everything in my power to make their companies more successful.

And guess what? Pretty soon I was getting orders and closing deals!

THE PHONE CALLS THAT RARELY GET MADE

The logic I discovered early in my career now seems so basic. Unfortunately, not many salespeople fully leverage the value of their existing customer base. Through the years, we've all made purchases of one type or another. We've shopped at local stores and purchased from a catalogue or over the Internet. Some of those purchases may have been small and some considerably larger. The one thing most of them have in common is the lack of follow-up by the person who made the sale.

Consider these calls I *should* have received from places where I did business.

"Hello, Mr. Heckman. You bought some golf shirts and a couple dozen balls in our pro shop a few weeks ago. How did you like them?"

I never got that call.

"Mr. Heckman, I see from our records that you entertained a group at our restaurant last week. How was the food and the service?"

Once again, no call.

"Hello, Mr. Heckman. You bought a car from me about two years ago. I hope you and your family are enjoying it. We appreciate your business. Please let me know how I can continue to provide you with good service."

I never got that call. Pity, because I shopped around the next time I needed a car, so he never heard from me.

"Hello. Mr. Heckman, I'm the real estate agent who sold you your home three years ago. I happened to drive by last week and saw that you've added a circular drive. The house looks great and I just wanted to let you know. If I can help you in the future, please let me know."

The real estate agent didn't follow up either.

So what's the point I'm making? When I need to sell my house, buy another car, take a group out to dinner, or buy some golf shirts, I have no *real loyalty* to whomever sold me the products and services in the first place. Why should I when they don't seem to care after the sale was made? Does that automatically mean I won't use their products or services again? That's a difficult question to answer. But I do know this. I *will* consider other companies and their products. Wouldn't you? Maybe someone else will make me feel like a valued customer!

Ignoring customers is the first (and perhaps worst) mistake made by salespeople. Let's examine why we make this blunder. Then we'll work on fixing the problem.

Why Don't We Follow Up?

I have purchased products and services throughout my personal and business life. However, I've received very few follow-up calls from salespeople.

So why don't we call back? In my experience, it comes down to just five key reasons.

◆ Many salespeople close a sale and move on to the next deal. They associate closing new business with the need to call on *new prospects*.

◆ Salespeople somehow assume existing customers will not need to be sold the product or service a second time. But even if that's true, the customer may know somebody who may be interested in their service. And that somebody may even be in the same company!

◆ The original salesperson has moved on, and the new salesperson does not know whom to call and doesn't have any personal history with that person or company.

◆ Many sales professionals lack the training and consistent direction from management to work the customer base. They simply don't follow up in a consistent and organized way.

◆ Finally, it takes time, effort, creativity, and a well-prepared plan. If you expect results from your follow-up efforts, you have to do it right, and do it consistently.

I think the 80/20 rule works in most businesses. You know, 80 percent of the business comes from 20 percent of the customers. Likewise, 80 percent of the profits come from 20 percent of your products or services. And so on. What's the point? By focusing on the "best customers," who are the 20 percent of the total market we might call on, we have huge leverage. This will help us sell more, gain references, and keep the competition out.

MIND SHARE . . . THE REAL REASON FOR FOLLOW-UP

If these are the reasons why salespeople don't follow up, here are reasons why we should.

People are creatures of habit. Research and common sense tell us that unless we are given a very good reason to change, we tend to stick to what has worked in the past.

We go back to our regular doctor, shop at the same grocery stores, and even drive the same route to work. It takes a powerful event to make most people change the way they have been doing things. So when it's time to make a purchase, it is usually the present supplier who gets the call.

The principle of Mind Share is as important as Market Share. It means that when a need comes up, the person or company who is "top of mind" will probably get a call. You've heard the phrase "out of sight, out of mind." Mind Share capitalizes on that notion by keeping a presence with the customer on a regular basis *after the sale*. The customer will get a call when another sales opportunity presents itself.

An organization getting good service, effective solutions, and value for their money will tend to stick with the current provider. If you keep them happy and stay in touch, in most cases they have no reason to switch to another provider.

This is why calling on current customers can and should be the most powerful weapon in your selling arsenal.

My thesis is simple: rather than grinding it out chasing unknown prospects and less-than-hot leads, you can double your sales by working your present client base.

How It's Done

OK, you're a believer. So how do you do it?

You do it by building fences around your best customers — fences made of hard work, a positive attitude, and an unstinting commitment to your clients. The fences serve two very important purposes. They keep you close to your customers, and they keep your competition at bay.

In the pages to follow, we'll hit these key elements in this customer-centric strategy:

◆ Serving clients well and ensuring that your support staff does as well

◆ Taking an ongoing, active, and honest interest in your client's success

◆ Staying in touch . . . remembering that Mind Share is critical in sales success

Based on my forty years of selling experience, these strategies work. So pick up your customer list and stop worrying about making cold calls!

The heart of what I hope you will learn from this book is simply this: existing customers are the single most valuable asset any sales organization can possess.

Chapter 2

I³: INTENT, INFORMATION, AND INSIGHT

The ultimate litmus test in the world of sales is whether or not your customers and prospects believe that you and your organization bring value to them. If they believe this, you'll have an opportunity to compete for the business. If not, you won't. It's that simple.

To demonstrate that you're capable of bringing value in a clear and practical way, you must cultivate and master I³, or Intent, Information, and Insight.

INTENT

Intent can be defined as the passionate commitment to the success of your client. That means instead of focusing on what they're trying to sell, great salespeople focus on what their clients really need in order to achieve success. It's a willingness to invest the time it takes to truly understand your customer's situation and what you and your company can do to bring value.

A quick way to think about the value you bring is to ask yourself these two simple, yet powerful questions: What problem can I help my customer solve? On what opportunity can I help them capitalize? Problems and opportunities; they are the Holy Grail.

Intent is thinking about your proposed solution . . . as it affects your customer's *total business*. In other words, we need to consider the impact our recommendation will have on all aspects of the business, not just the day-to-day operations. Certainly it would be beneficial to improve speed in manufacturing or to collect accounts receivable faster. But we need to extend the value chain beyond simply an internal look and ask ourselves, "If my prospect takes this action, what's the impact internally *and* on his or her customers? In fact, what's the impact on the prospect's vendors or business partners as well?" We can even extend our thinking to include the impact on the customer's competitors. OK, you get the idea. Intent is about customer success and extending your thinking outside the box to include all aspects of the business.

When Do We Declare Victory?

Intent means working to deploy your company's capabilities, skills, and resources on behalf of your clients or prospects. It means you're sincere about your clients' success and feel that *only* when they succeed, you succeed.

The simplest way to understand how your prospect or client determines success is to ask, "How will you and management measure the success of this decision?" There it is, very direct and to the point. Not only do you and your prospect need to discuss success, but it's a great qualifying question as well. If there isn't a clear understanding of the end game, it's going to be very difficult to determine value beyond low price.

A client's answer may align perfectly with your view of the world and that's good. It's obviously the outcome we wanted. On the other hand, the answer *may not* be what you would have guessed or is not in sync with your past experience. In the spirit of Intent, you must *positively confront* the issue and clarify what you heard. By offering additional information based on your experience, you can discuss the subject candidly and attempt to get a collaborative picture of success.

"Kelly, I'm interested in understanding how you decided that an internal rate of return on a project like this can achieve 30 percent. Our experience suggests that it is more typically in the range of 15 percent to 20 percent. What am I overlooking?"

There, you've got it out on the table in a positive way. As the discussion continues, you may gain the Insight you need to adjust your thinking, or, you may be in a position that calls for a tough decision . . . Can you truly deliver the results Kelly is expecting? Remember the overarching goal. We are Intent on our client's success and must be certain that we are in agreement on expectations. In fact, even if we are not the right organization to deliver the solution, we should admit it and offer suggestions that may be better for them.

Painting the Picture of Success

Here's an example of positive confrontation and then collaboration, all in the spirit of Intent. A customer wanted to move forward on the installation of a new office system and roll it out companywide. In addition, they wanted to do it over a three-day weekend. That was the definition of success. My experience told me it was the wrong approach. It was too much change for the organization to absorb all at once. The company was very administratively dependent, it would have serious customer service issues if there were any glitches in the installation. For the system to be effectively implemented, the company would have to offer training and individual assistance to its employees. Did I want to get the systems installed and move on to other opportunities? Yes. However, it wasn't in my customer's best interest, so I confronted the issue directly.

I suggested that we do the installation in three phases, spread over forty-five days. I further suggested that we pick two departments with strong managers for Phase One. We discussed it thoroughly and agreed that we would do the installation based on performance. We agreed that we would ask the department managers for Phase One to be advocates for the new system. Every organization has an informal communication system commonly called the "grapevine," and we felt that subsequent phases would go more smoothly when they heard good things about Phase One.

So the Picture of Success was redrawn based on the Intent to help the client be successful. Once that Picture of Success is developed, it must be shared with key people in *both* companies so everyone understands the commitment being made.

Speaking with the Locals

Let's look outside the business world for an example to drive home the importance of Intent. Last year we signed up for a biking tour of the Tuscany region of Italy. In my desire to avoid being "the ugly American," I mentioned to our travel agent that we were going to listen to language tapes prior to the trip. She quickly suggested that while the tapes could be helpful, it would make more sense to concentrate on a few key phrases which would be more useful to us on a daily basis, like how to order food or ask for directions. She said she would e-mail them to us so that we could practice at home and volunteered to help us over the phone if we thought that would help as well.

Her Intent was for our trip to go well. It would have been easy for her to simply agree with our idea of listening to tapes and then go back to selling other travel services. Instead, she applied her experience with busy people and suggested a different Picture of Success. The outcome was a fun trip and an appreciation for our travel agent's genuine Intent to be helpful.

Listening to the Experts

In his powerful business seminars, Dr. Mahan Khalsa says our Intent should not be to sell but to help our clients succeed. That advice echoes well-known speaker Zig Ziglar's observation that "the best way to get what you want is to help a lot of other people get what they want."

Certainly the quality of your product or service is critical in helping clients succeed. There are also other ways to show Intent. For instance, introducing a customer to a business associate of yours who can be helpful is showing Intent. Simply mentioning the quality of product your customer manufactures when the opportunity presents itself also shows Intent. Perhaps identifying a good candidate for a job opening is the value-add. Should you earn a fee when you do these things? Nope. Your reward will come through stronger relationships with people who can say "Yes" or "No" to important decisions.

The Customer of My Customer

When my partner and I started our first company years ago, our attorney Bill French helped with the many legal instruments required to be in business. He did a good job. We paid his invoices and began building the business. A couple of months later, Bill called to see if we could have lunch with the president of a local company. He explained that since both of us called on the banking community, we might have services we could provide each other. Bill's Intent was to help our business and it was appreciated. There was no need to consider another law firm when we needed legal assistance. Bill French was our lawyer because he delivered good value—and he cared about our business!

In another example, the Chief Executive Officer (CEO) of a large services company asked if I would mind interviewing a candidate he was considering as Chief Financial Officer. He wanted the viewpoint of an informed outsider and approached me because he felt I was familiar with his organization. I was glad to help and conducted the interview. Did I receive a fee for my services? No, because I'm not in the executive search business, but I *am interested* in helping my client be successful. By the way, as a bonus, it sure didn't hurt my rapport with the CEO!

INFORMATION

If Intent is the commitment to think and act in the client's best interest and to help them succeed, then Information is the vital link between Intent and fulfillment.

Imagine for a moment coming down with flu-like symptoms and going to a local medical clinic for help. But before you see a physician or nurse, the receptionist poses the following question as she holds up a syringe for your inspection.

"We usually charge forty-five dollars for this injection, but it's on special today for fifteen!"

Hold on a minute! We haven't even been examined. Where are the X-rays or the blood workup? Don't they usually hand the patient a little bottle and point to the restroom? Where's the doctor?!

You would be appalled, and rightly so. Yet that is precisely the cart-before-the-horse approach taken by many aspiring sales professionals. All too often, I've seen salespeople start pitching their products before they've even examined their prospects' situations or have any real insight into their problems or opportunities. That's not just a poor selling strategy. It can earn you a quick and permanent exit from your client's or prospect's office.

You want a doctor to diagnose your illness using the most accurate and updated information available, and combine that with experience. And you want that done before prescribing a treatment! Likewise, executives expect you to know something— quite a few things, really—about their business, and in some cases about the executives as individuals, before you propose a solution.

Do you remember when you were growing up, and you heard one or both of your parents say something like, "You've got to do your homework to get ahead!" Guess what? Mom and Dad were right!

The Basics of Information

Basic research is no great mystery and it's not that difficult. If your target is a public company, it takes just five minutes to call the company's investor relations department to request a standard information package containing their annual report, 10(K) report, product literature, press releases, and transcripts of recent speeches. It might take fifteen to twenty minutes to read and quickly digest the material.

You're looking for industry trends and the company's performance as viewed by their executives, stock market analysts, and industry watchers, to name a few. This "grounding in reality" forms the basis of Information required to be helpful to decision makers.

Next, visit the company Web site as well as the Web sites of the industry analysts who track the company. You can usually get the names of the brokerage firms and the industry analysts from the investor relations department of the company you're researching. They are very aware of the analysts who monitor the company and may even send you recent reports. It's also a good idea to obtain Information from other industry analysts so that you have a well-rounded perspective on the company and its competitive situation.

What we want initially is to understand how the company is positioning itself and what the stock market analysts are saying about both the company and the industry. It might take fifteen minutes to browse those sites and to summarize the key messages.

Remember, we are mining for gold nuggets: those performance-based gems of Information that are of key interest to senior management. As a general guideline, you only do this on high-value, high-potential accounts, and as we've just seen, you can do it in less than thirty minutes.

Here's the Good News

Once you've done the basic research and have a sense of the important Information, it's easy to keep yourself updated on any changes and take quick action. You'll also have Insight into the changes based on your research and understanding of the industry and the company.

For example, a large retailer, the Gap, announced the hiring of two executive vice presidents. One was brought in to head up supply chain and logistics. The other was announced as the new Chief Information Officer (CIO). Interestingly enough, one came from outside the clothing business while the other had worked with the Gap CEO a few years before. Time to research both new players and prepare for a lot of change at the Gap!

Researching Privately-Owned Companies

Start with the Internet. Most companies have a Web site containing descriptions of the organization, its products and services, company locations, press releases, biographies of key people, and other vital information.

In addition to Web site information, most major cities have publications devoted to the local business scene. Many have lists of the twenty-five largest companies in a variety of industries; all are displayed with the names of key people and their phone numbers. Your target may be included in the list.

Private companies often speak at industry events and at activities like chamber of commerce luncheons and other gatherings. The talks can provide valuable Information and Insight. In addition, when you call for an appointment, you can refer to the fact that you heard the speech the president of the company recently made to an industry group.

Finally, don't overlook your own network of friends and associates. Suppliers to and customers of the target company can provide Information that could prove valuable. There's a good possibility that people you know will be familiar with the company. If so, ask them for input, and in return be generous with Insight on companies with whom you're familiar.

Once again, you're trying to gain access to Information about your potential customer's business model, how they go to market, the quality of their products and services, who they do business with, and the problems and opportunities the target organization has, based on others in the same industry segment.

You won't have all the Information you'd like on a private company since they're not required to report such things as financial results. You will have to get additional Information by talking with the company first hand. But bear in mind your conversations will be far more meaningful if you've done the homework step first.

When you gather Information before making a prospect call, you will begin to get a feel for whether they really are a prospect at all.

How Deep to Dig

How much research is enough?

That depends on the companies you are targeting, the cost and complexity of your solution, and how likely a prospect they may be based on your experience.

If you are offering a good price on office supplies to an office manager, you can probably hop in your car and go make the sale with a minimum of preparation. But if you are proposing a mission-critical enterprise software system to the CIO of a Fortune 1000 company, you had better be prepared to take the time and effort to understand the implications of the possible decision—through the prospects' eyes.

As a general rule, it's better to have more data points than you need rather than appearing ill prepared. Remember, though, it's not about spouting facts. At this point in the sales cycle, it's about validating what you've learned and gaining new Insight. It usually takes a little longer to prepare for the first call than for subsequent calls but once you get into the habit, you'll better define what you need and where to find it.

It's All in the Math

Astute salespeople will try to calculate the potential return on any sale, and then invest in their research accordingly.

The Information you gather initially and during the first couple of calls will help you determine how much time and effort it will take to get in a position to convert your investment into business booked.

You're really asking yourself if the ultimate prize warrants getting the needed internal approvals, writing a proposal, or answering a Request for Proposal (RFP). You may have to sell your manager on securing tough delivery dates or using a highly-valued, but very busy, technical specialist.

Is it worth it? If you do your homework first and gather the right Information, you'll be able to prioritize your opportunities according to facts. This will enable you to apply your scarce resources on the best opportunities and avoid chasing every potential deal with equal ferocity.

Business Drivers

What motivates a business to buy?

There are key business metrics and measurements all businesses monitor. When they deviate from expectations, senior managers start losing sleep. That's because those metrics reflect the trends, market forces, and business activities which ultimately determine the health of the company. Business drivers aren't limited to "for profit" companies. Government and not-for-profit organizations have performance drivers as well.

Fundamental business drivers can include issues such as these:

◆ Weak Financial Performance

◆ Customer Service Issues

◆ Government Compliance

◆ Key Employee Attrition

◆ Need for New Technology

◆ Globalization

◆ Availability of Capital

◆ Product Quality

◆ Labor Issues

◆ Acquisition Integration

◆ Market Leadership

◆ Shipping Market Share

Your basic research will help you uncover the critical business drivers that must be addressed by your client or prospect. Once you understand these drivers, you can validate them with the organization and begin to map your solutions to them.

Know the Person

Whenever possible, you should research and prepare for the "type" of person you will be meeting.

Some companies make decisions by consensus, while others are filled with renaissance thinkers who thrive on individual initiative. Technical managers are probably interested in how things work, the processes involved, and the infrastructure required. Executives may want new ideas, Return on Investment (ROI) models, and a deeper understanding of what other business leaders are doing to improve performance.

Other factors are important as well. A person sixty years old and nearing retirement may offer a very different decision-making profile than a person who is thirty-five and trying to make his or her mark. The same applies to a person who has been at a company for twenty-five years versus someone recruited the previous month from a high-powered competitor and who was brought in to "shake things up."

You can glean some of this information from the public sources we talked about earlier. If a friend or associate knows the person, call and ask about your prospect's reputation as well as his or her style and background, how he or she does business, and if possible, something about your prospect's personal life, such as outside interests, family situation, or involvement in charity work.

Overkill? Not in my experience. You simply cannot know enough about the people involved in the ultimate decision, whether that means signing the contract or influencing it. With the right Information, you'll be able to tightly target your messages and be viewed as resourceful and a quick study.

Know Thyself

Before you hit the road, you should also take a hard look in the mirror.

In addition to selling your product or service, you are also selling yourself. If your prospect perceives you to be uninformed, disorganized, or unkempt, it will hurt your ability to generate meaningful conversation, thus limiting your access in the future. During those initial few minutes of a meeting, you are modeling how you and your company do business through your presence, knowledge, behavior, and communication skills.

So be aware that your "personal packaging," your appearance, your behavior, your confidence, and your overall demeanor can affect your success. Your dress and grooming, how you listen, your diction and grammar, even how you shake hands will affect how people perceive you. So think seriously about these things because your prospects certainly will. In fact, they're probably asking themselves if they would introduce you to their boss, a peer, or even a subordinate. Will their introduction of you be something they will have to explain later?

It may help to seek the frank advice of people you trust, including co-workers, family, and friends. Ask them how you come across; ask what they see as your strengths and your weaknesses. Don't be defensive. Listen. And always look for ways to improve yourself and your personal presentation. Remember, you don't have to be "fast on your feet" or a whiz at formal presentations to be successful. But you must look, act, and convey a professional image to sell in the offices of decision makers.

Is image really that important? Based on my work with decision makers, it is. I'm not suggesting you have to look like a Hollywood star or dress as though you have just stepped out of a fashion magazine. I am suggesting that just as packaging is important to a product on the shelf at the grocery store, your personal packaging is critical as well.

A good friend of mine, and a seasoned sales executive, said, only a little in jest, "You don't get a haircut from a barber with bad-looking hair—or seek nutritional advice from the Krispy Kreme Donut Shop manager!" In other words, you are a big factor in building confidence and trust by the way you handle yourself and deal with people.

I was told by my first sales manager that I had a great smile, but in business situations I maintained a rather solemn, and at times, somber look. *Exactly,* I thought, *business is serious.* But his point was made. You can be very serious about business and yet be engaging during the meeting by smiling, gesturing, and relaxing just a bit.

Put Yourself in Their Place

The truly great salespeople don't ask themselves whether or not they will make their quota. Rather, they ask themselves what they can do to make life simpler, more productive, and more profitable for their customers and prospects. As we discussed earlier, the Intent is to help our clients and prospects be successful.

Lou Holtz, one of football's most successful coaches, does a lot of public speaking. At a recent speech to a group of business leaders, he suggested that decision makers have a short list of questions that they ask themselves very early in the first meeting. The questions are: Do they know what they're talking about? Is it relevant to me and my situation? Can I trust them? Can they perform?

This approach requires that you adopt a consultative mindset, one that is focused on the perceptions, needs, and expectations of your prospect. One good way to evaluate your own performance is to imagine the prospect asking these pointed questions:

- ◆ How well does the salesperson really understand my unique situation?

- ◆ Do they know what they're talking about? How do I *know* they do?

- ◆ Will their solution work for me? How do I know?

- ◆ Do I trust these people and believe what they say?

- ◆ Can I see building a relationship with them and their company?

- ◆ How will I feel when they meet the executives of my company?

Put yourself in your prospect's shoes and answer these tough questions. If you don't have the right answers, you've got some work to do.

Is Information the ultimate sales weapon? Yes, especially when combined with Intent and Insight!

INSIGHT

Insight is crucial for becoming a great salesperson. Before we can help prospects or customers, we must first understand their current and past performances, their current situations and the challenges they're facing. With that Information, we then craft a set of solutions and chart a path that connects the two. Insight means more than assembling a binder full of facts. It requires good thinking, sound judgment, tapping into the experience of others, and the ability to listen.

Let's be honest, developing Insight also takes hard work and commitment. Many salespeople are not willing to make the effort. As we observed when we discussed the Information we gain from our research and homework, it takes time and diligence. But the great salespeople take that time to gain the vital

Insight needed to solve problems and capture opportunities for the prospect or customer.

In this book, and particularly in the Tool Kit, we'll examine how you can gain valuable Insight into your customer's problems and opportunities. We'll discuss the metrics companies use to track and evaluate performance. You'll identify the sources to consult for solid Information on almost any company or organization.

Who's Getting It Right?

So what are the elements of Insight? Business leaders expect you to know the basics: their industry, their company, and how your products or services might help their performance. That basic knowledge is mandatory. There's no magic; it's expected. You know it and they know it.

So far you're doing what's expected. Now let's see how Insight will separate you from the pack. Insight is understanding what high-performing companies in other industries are doing as market leaders. This Insight, often called Best Practices, allows you to pick the very best examples from other companies and directly apply them to your client's situation. The key here is relevancy. Can your client or prospect identify with the examples you present? Is there respect for the companies you've selected to showcase?

Today's business leaders monitor high-performing companies regardless of industry. That's probably the reason so many companies have adopted General Electric's Six Sigma quality program and Economic Value Added (EVA) approaches to managing their businesses. Just watch the industry press when Wal-Mart makes an announcement about a new initiative. You don't have to be doing business with General Electric or Wal-Mart for your Best Practices to gain interest. Well-run companies of any size can serve as good examples. It's the keen Insight you have into what made them so successful that will allow you to fine-tune and tailor the Best Practices to exactly fit your prospects and their unique requirements and cultures.

Insight in Practice

At an advanced stage, Insight moves to asking questions that may address the problem or opportunity from a different, even oblique angle. For example, companies of all sizes are wrestling with the concept of outsourcing various business functions. The fundamental notion is to save money by using the experts to perform the work, and thus return management's focus to critical activities, not on lower-priority activities.

Critical thinking and industry Insight allowed IBM to develop the concept of activity-based usage of technology, with a corresponding pricing structure. Did they hit a market nerve with the approach? Yes, based on the media coverage and analyst comments. It's very likely that their competitors are spending a lot of time and energy determining their strategy. Where did IBM's Insight come from? From talking to prospects and customers, and probably from looking at pricing practices from other industries. Will it be a success? The jury is still out; it looks very interesting. The new approach may not be right for everyone. So now there is an option. The prospect can consider the new utility pricing model or buy from IBM in the traditional manner! Clever thinking indeed.

Not So Fast on That Acquisition!

Another example of Insight occurred when our sales team was presenting to a large consumer packaged-goods client. We were in Phoenix and had the CEO and his direct reports for a ninety-minute presentation concerning process improvement. We knew it was competitive and that the CEO was known to dominate most discussions.

We knew our subject well. We had a lot of experience with other consumer product organizations and felt strongly that our solution would generate considerable cost savings and improve customer service. Part of the process improvement was in the order entry area, and we knew the names of most of their larger customers who would benefit from improvements in this area.

As we prepared for the presentation, it was evident that we needed to grab the attention of the executive group quickly. They had a short attention span, exacerbated by the dominant CEO. Our research gave us two keen pieces of Insight. First, the largest store chain in the world had decided on a new paperless approach to order entry. They planned to make it optional initially but then make it mandatory in order to remain a "preferred supplier," a very critical designation to its vendor community.

Second, we discovered that the executive team was highly compensated through salaries and bonuses. However, their individual equity and stock option ownership was at the low end of the industry. The company's stock price was low and they were a clear takeover candidate due to their strong balance sheet and established brands. In the event of a takeover, the executive team could well lose their jobs, depending on the strategy of the acquirer. If that happened, the large salaries and bonuses would go away, and the payoff on the equity and options for the senior management team would be low.

Based on those two nuggets of Insight, we modified the opening of our presentation. We gained the Insight from the online sources available and by digesting the company's 10(K) and financial reports. In addition, we talked to our retail practice partners to learn about the new order entry initiative coming from the market leader, which our prospect would have to address.

Before we cranked up the PowerPoint presentation, we introduced our team and stated clearly that our Intent was to use the Information and Insight we had gained in two areas important to them, both as executives *and* shareholders. The announcement of the order entry initiative caused eyes to turn to the CEO. The CEO asked how long it would take to meet the new requirement. There was considerable foot shuffling and vague answers. Our Insight had hit a hot button!

When we talked about the share price being low and the possibility of the company being acquired, the CEO slapped his hand on the desk. "That's exactly what I've been saying! So how does your proposed solution help us improve performance?"

There you have it: the power and logic of Intent, Information, and Insight. Our Intent was absolutely to make our client successful. We gathered the vital Information to really understand the complete picture. Finally, we looked beyond the obvious and brought Insight into the equation. We clinched the deal and were awarded a sole-source contract for five years! It remains the largest single contract I've personally been involved with . . . and it continues to be a source of great pride. Would we have gotten the contract without the Insight we learned? Maybe, but why take the chance?

We're on a Roll, so Let's Look at Two More

I was asked by my client to debrief the loss of a contract at a giant insurance company. My client had lost the potential engagement to one of its competitors. The president of the insurance company was blunt in his assessment.

"You answered the proposal well enough," he said, "but given your people, your experience, and your reputation, we quite frankly thought you would have brought us something more."

The RFP had been answered, but the rules of Intent and Insight weren't applied, so the business was lost. The Intent, as it appeared to the life insurance company, was to answer the proposal. But there was little indication that my client planned to apply their considerable resources to make the prospect's business even more successful. In addition, they didn't show compelling Insight during the final presentation.

That Insight should have demonstrated exactly how the solution answered the problems and opportunities the client faced in the overall business, not just the information technology issues being addressed. They also lacked examples from outside the insurance industry that the decision makers could relate to and find valuable. Examples could have come from the banking industry or capital markets firms. Applying technology to such marketing activities as data mining (to find additional opportunities with current customers) or discussing tools used by call centers (to launch and track direct marketing activities) would have been good examples. Insight is about going beyond responding to an RFP. It's about new ideas that solve problems or drive opportunities in a compelling way.

The Machine Works, but Will My Customers Care?

During the early days of the ATM (automated teller machine), financial institutions began making large investments in this new, revolutionary, twenty-four-hour service. I was working for Docutel, the inventor of the ATM, and we had a prospect in the Southeast. We also had two larger competitors fighting for the business.

Our Intent was to make our banking customer successful in installing ATMs and seeing strong customer acceptance. We could handle the installation, but our Insight into the market suggested that some of the first banks to install ATMs were facing reluctant customers and usage was low. Change is always difficult, and using an ATM back then was a major change for consumers.

Based on that Insight, we brought in a highly respected advertising agency. You might ask at this point what an advertising agency would know about using an ATM, and you would be right to ask. They didn't have experience in selling ATMs, but they sure knew how to position a new product or service with the consumer.

The agency discussed the experience they had in dealing with consumer products companies and in the retail industry. They presented samples of the work they had done in positioning a product or service successfully. One of their suggestions was to have a demographically-matched group of ATM demonstrators on site to assist the bank's customers. In other words, a college town would have a younger staff demonstrating the ATMs, and where the demographics were older, a more mature staff would be available to answer questions and provide training.

In addition, the agency suggested clever names for the ATM program to give it a personality and avoid the perception of "automation" or "Big Brother is watching." It worked, and *Tillie the Teller* was successfully introduced in the Atlanta market. It became one of the fastest-growing ATM programs in the United States.

Our Insight was simply that a winning ATM program was not about how the computer in the ATM worked, but about gaining and retaining customer interest. We were able to change the game and win a very large ATM contract based on Intent and Insight.

Insight . . . Simply Stated

Once you've gathered and reviewed the Information available, true Insight would ask, "Now what, and, so what!?" It's going the next step to add personal experience, best practices, and "what if" discussions with smart people. This exercise will help you develop solutions and approaches that aren't obvious to you, the prospect . . . or the competition!

SUMMARY

◆ Intent is a true and passionate commitment to the success of your client or prospect.

◆ The assumption is that you will be rewarded with an opportunity to do business now or in the future if you display true Intent with the client or prospect.

◆ You will be modeling Intent throughout the sales cycle by your attitude, actions, recommendations, and follow-up. How you sell sends a strong signal about how you will do business after the sale.

◆ Information and Insight provide relevant and high-impact discussion points. It shows that you've invested time and effort in understanding how to match your solutions to the prospect's unique requirements.

◆ Information is pervasive in today's information-driven world. Insight is what allows you to use that Information to solve problems or capture opportunities for the prospect. By applying different and interesting approaches and perspectives based on your experience and expertise to the situation, your prospect benefits from your Insight.

◆ Systematic use of Intent, Information, and Insight will differentiate you from "product-driven" competitors who focus on *their* product or service. As Dr. Stephen Covey states, "Seek first to understand before being understood."

Chapter 3

UNIQUECONNECT

We were conducting a sales workshop for Accenture, a large consulting firm, a couple of years ago. Two things made the session memorable. First, it was held in Vail, Colorado, during the height of ski season. Truly a teaching challenge at its best! How would we keep the attendees from the slopes? There was a simple answer to that challenge. We started at 6:00 a.m. and finished each day at noon . . . then off to the ski lifts!

The second thing happened when we were brainstorming ideas about how to set up appointments with decision makers. We talked about the challenges of getting through an assistant, whether or not to leave a voice mail, and what to say if the decision maker happened to answer the phone.

The attendees were convinced that "cold calling" was tough, and the discussion that day confirmed it. True enough. Cold calling isn't easy, or, terribly productive. Finally someone said,

"What we need is a connection with the person we're trying to see. We need a *UniqueConnect!*"

That simple phrase says it all. We wanted to "connect" in a "unique way." We wanted to cut through the maze and frustration of getting an appointment with someone we may not know well, if at all. As we continued to work on the idea of Unique-Connect, it was clear that the notion worked for both customer *and* prospect calls.

A Defining Term

A UniqueConnect is a relationship, referral, or piece of information that helps establish an immediate and positive link between you and the customer or prospect. Some UniqueConnects are obvious and fairly easy to uncover. For example, you may call on a current customer to tell him about a new product. If you know each other and have a relationship, then your chances for an appointment are strengthened as a result.

Other UniqueConnects are earned through research and hard work. For instance, you have researched a company and found that the person you want to see used to work for one of your current customers. Of course, some UniqueConnects are considerably stronger than others.

Without question, *the strongest UniqueConnect* is a *personal referral* to the decision maker you want to meet. However, while this is ideal, it doesn't happen often enough to be the only UniqueConnect that you need to consider.

UniqueConnects, ranked in order of impact, include:

♦ **Those within the organization.** An introduction from a current customer to a "new prospect" within their organization. The prospect might be in another division or location. This UniqueConnect is powerful because of the Insight and Information you have about the customer, the service you provided, and your mutual experience of working together.

◆ **Alumni.** Get an introduction from a current customer to someone with whom they used to work before changing jobs or careers. Smart companies have cultivated strong alumni programs to stay close to former associates.

◆ **An outside referral.** A referral from a satisfied customer to someone at another company. There is a strong likelihood that the new prospect will take your call due to their relationship with your contact.

◆ **High-impact Insight.** Use valuable Insight or Information you have developed about the prospect's company, industry, or competitive situation. You determine, for example, that your product can reduce "re-works" in manufacturing based on actual client experience. You couple that with the stated goal of your prospect to improve overall quality . . . and you have a UniqueConnect.

◆ **New product, idea, or solution.** A new offering with compelling benefits for the prospect can be converted into a UniqueConnect. This is particularly true when you have clear, supporting metrics to prove the business case.

◆ **Mutual customers or business relationships.** Who doesn't want help selling their products and services? Using your network of business relationships can be valuable to your prospects in their marketing and sales efforts. An offer to introduce them to a business colleague of yours can be a UniqueConnect.

◆ **Industry or business Insight.** Introduce an industry or market research report or article that you really think your prospect will find interesting.

Much of what you will read in this book revolves around the creation, nurturing, and leveraging of UniqueConnects. Tom McQuaid, a longtime friend and successful businessman, once told me, "Without a bridge to the prospect, selling is tough!" I couldn't agree more and have found UniqueConnect to be that bridge.

As a rule of thumb, ask yourself this question before every sales call: "What is my UniqueConnect in this situation?" If the answer is, "I don't really have one," you must question your ability to have impact with this prospect.

The UniqueConnect approach separates great salespeople from the struggling also-rans.

PUTTING UNIQUECONNECT TO WORK

Most Valued Assets

Organizations invest in a wide variety of assets. The list is long: from buildings and production equipment, right down to desks, chairs, and staplers. But there is one asset without which organizations cannot hope to succeed, and that's human capital—great employees and great customers.

Human capital in the form of great employees is the subject for another book. We want to concentrate on human capital—the customers and organizations doing business with us now or have in the past.

Customers feed the business engine. They pay the bills, fuel your growth, and drive every good business plan. If you have satisfied customers, you can survive the downturns and keep your competition at bay. Whether times are good and everyone is in the buying mode or when business is awful, customers are our first order of business.

With that in mind, let's first examine the strategies and tools you can use to increase your sales by better serving, selling, and leveraging your relationships with existing customers. Once we have a solid plan for customers, we'll transition to finding prospects through our UniqueConnect strategy.

Building Big Fences around Customers

There are two broad types of clients—active and inactive. In either case you have a clear UniqueConnect; they are or were customers. The only real difference between developing a strategy for active and inactive customers is to find out why someone has become inactive. Has the original decision maker moved on? Has a competitor spent more time in developing the relationship? Were they a "one-time buyer" and simply didn't need any more of your products or services? Was there a bad experience with the product or service? Once you've established whether an inactive customer can be resurrected, you can move forward.

Obviously, customers represent potential business. Everyone will vigorously nod their heads and agree that current customers offer potential, in some cases, great potential. It's almost the Holy Grail of selling.

However, we agreed earlier that many salespeople do not have ongoing relationships with many of the people and companies they have done business with in the past. After purchasing homes, cars, personal computers, and so forth, you rarely have an ongoing relationship with the salesperson or the company because they did not have a proactive plan to stay in touch and continue to serve you and your company.

They sold, you bought, the bill was paid, and that was it. So when the need for a new purchase came up, you didn't automatically call the past supplier. They had little or no Mind Share with you and the chance for a sale vanished or went to a competitor.

Perhaps I'm being too harsh. Maybe you were sent a J. D. Powers survey about your car buying experience or there was a comment card at the checkout desk at the hotel asking how your stay was, but rarely is there follow-up from the salesperson or the organization months after the sale was made.

Follow-up Strategies

So what are the key areas for follow-up that will strengthen your UniqueConnect, build customer loyalty, keep the competition at arms length, and keep you "top of mind" with your customers? Here are several to consider:

◆ **How have our products/services performed for you?** It's that simple. But you've got to do it more than once, shortly after the purchase. It must be ongoing, and it must be sincere. If you want customers to be satisfied, you must be prepared to listen and to solve problems, if necessary.

◆ **What results have you had since your decision?** Remember, people buy to solve problems or capture an opportunity. So how has your product or service performed against expectations? The answers will provide tremendous Insight into customer satisfaction and will offer new opportunities for letting prospects know what they can expect by doing business with you, based on actual results. Having worked with some of the world's most sophisticated companies, I am convinced salespeople don't ask this question nearly often enough. When I ask clients if they have customers we can quote, many times they have difficulty coming up with case studies or references who have hard data or metrics to show their Return on Investment (ROI). You've got to ask customers about their results to gain Insight and understanding about the value of your products and services. "On time, on budget" doesn't cut it anymore. Actual measurable results do!

◆ **Future plans.** This one is a little trickier. Once your customers know that you honestly care about their success, the conversation can move to the future. It's human nature to share Information and future needs with someone who listens and has proven he or she will take meaningful action to bring results, even if it's long after the initial sale.

◆ **Ideas, Information, and Insight!** Personal experience and many discussions with decision makers confirm that bringing customers new ideas, Information, and Insight is of high value. The key guideline is that you must have done your homework and filtered out the best ideas and Information for each specific customer. It's not about stacks of information, it's about relevant Information. And don't restrict the flow of Information to just their industry. Leaders like to know what other leaders are doing and how to capitalize on new, fresh ideas and Insight.

Connecting the Dots

By developing a meaningful follow-up strategy, you've earned the right to ask for introductions to others in the company who could benefit from your services. In addition, there may be introductions within industry groups and with business associates. Once a salesperson has mastered the art of consistent follow-up and delivered real value, referrals are a natural extension of the relationship. Don't you do it in your own life? I know I refer people and companies who have both performed and followed up. I should receive a commission from USAA for the number of times I've lauded their financial services and products, but they've really earned it through world-class service, not self-promotion!

The journey to UniqueConnect selling begins by working closely with current customers and making certain that their investment in your services *and you* is valuable to them.

FIVE RULES FOR CLIENTS

First Rule: Serve Them Well!

Serve well. That's the cardinal rule for successful companies in every industry. That means you live up to, or better yet, exceed what you said you would do in terms of performance, quality, and value.

Of course, salespeople can't control all of those variables, but you can care about everything that affects your customers and act as ambassadors between your company and the client organization.

Work to position yourself, in the minds of your customers, as the "go-to source" for your company. As the go-to source, you've got to be prepared for both popular and unpopular situations. It's easy to be the go-to person when they want to order another dozen widgets. It's tough when a delivery is postponed or a service call doesn't get handled right the first time. Finger-pointing at some other department or person doesn't happen if you're truly the go-to source.

I know many sales professionals who drive home the point of being responsive by writing their cell phone numbers and maybe even their home phone numbers on their business cards. It's a simple way of saying, "Call me when you need me." They'll also provide a knowledgable "back-up" person's name in case they are not available.

Second Rule: Stay in Touch

If the first step with clients is to serve well, then the second step in "relationship building" with your clients is to stay in touch on a consistent, but not invasive, basis.

You should set up a program designed to keep a presence with the customer in order to monitor the pulse of the relationship. Some companies use sophisticated software tools to track such efforts. While very useful and particularly important to the management of your company, the key is not record keeping, but client contact.

In the Tool Kit section of this book, we'll look at proven tools such as the Relationship Map and discuss how to strengthen your relationships with key client contacts.

Remember, all things being equal or close to being equal, people prefer to do business where they have personal relationships. In other words, if your product or service is equal to or very close to being equal, you may win the business if you have a strong relationship with the decision maker. Yes, personal relationships can be the strongest competitive advantage!

Building a positive relationship is not about overtly pitching new business. Of course you would like to sell more business, but you really want to use these periodic opportunities to determine your client's level of satisfaction, to assess the return they are getting on their investment, to understand their future needs, and to identify and address potential problems.

Third Rule: Take Time to Touch Base

Through the years I've often picked up my cell phone or used a public phone to call a few clients and simply say, "I was thinking about you and wanted to call. How are you doing?" The world moves fast and can get very impersonal. So when a person takes just a little time to say hello it can have a favorable impact. It says that they're important to you and that you care about the relationship and their success.

The phone call doesn't always have to be around business. It can encompass anything that you know is important to your customer. I have a client who must be Notre Dame's biggest football fan. Occasionally before a big game I'll call to wish him luck; we both know he's not playing on Saturday, but he takes his football that seriously!

At the end of the day when you've finished your e-mails, take a moment and forward an interesting piece of information you found on the Web to a couple of business associates. Add a short introduction like, "Saw this and thought of you. Enjoy the article, and let's get together for coffee soon."

Great sales professionals take the time to expand and enhance their UniqueConnects with customers and prospects. I make it a matter of habit to contact at least five customers every week by either phone or e-mail. And I try to include some piece of business or personal information I think they'll find interesting.

Fourth Rule: Prospect within Current Clients

If handled correctly, these customer contact calls will naturally lead to additional sales opportunities. That most often happens when your clients talk about future activities such as new product rollouts, expansion plans, and staffing changes.

It's natural to discuss other areas of their businesses that could benefit from your services. Internal introductions are critical in "working a client." Who better to help you tell your story about the good work you've done for one department of a company than the very person who made the decision?

In the Tools Section of this book, we talk about the 3 X 3 Model for networking within a client company. This strategy will keep you from being locked in with just one decision maker. It will also earn you a positive introduction to other potential buyers based on your relationship with one of their peers. As a general rule of thumb, you can't know too many people in a customer organization. You build a constituency and gain Insight at the same time. Not a bad investment of time and energy.

Fifth Rule: Develop a Referral Network

Existing customers can be an excellent source of referrals to other companies. Virtually every businessperson has contacts with businesses, vendors, previous employers, friends, and civic and social organizations. These are powerful sources of new sales targets.

But most salespeople do a poor job of tapping into these sales referrals.

"Who else do you know who might benefit from my services?" is a question I've heard asked all too many times. This approach forces your customers to put themselves in your shoes and try and come up with prospects that fit your business model. That's a lot to ask.

Here's a better way:

Why not prime the pump by naming one or two target companies where you hope to get an appointment, and then ask your customer if they know anyone there. It's even better if you have the names of the people you want to meet at those organizations, your customer may know them or know someone who does.

By taking a little time to research the prospect's Web site, you can learn the names of key executives. That could mean a UniqueConnect just waiting to happen when you mention those names to your client.

This approach takes the onus off your client. Even if they don't know anyone at those companies, you have identified the type of prospect you are looking for. This may spark a referral to a company you had not thought of before.

The golden rule with regard to referrals is to always let the person making the referral know the outcome. A quick phone call, a handwritten note, or an e-mail is an effective way of saying, "Thanks." This feedback simply says that you took action and appreciate the assistance. My experience indicates that when you "close the loop" with the person making the referral they will think of another one for you to call.

PROSPECTS

Break New Ground

You can boost sales significantly by focusing your efforts on current customers. It is important to build strong relationship fences around your customers. This is even truer for customers with the highest potential. You will keep earning the right to do more business with them by serving them well, concentrating on their success, working the relationship, and being attentive.

Yet, no matter how good you are and how hard you work, existing customers may not keep your sales pipeline filled. Client needs will change. People move on. Your competitors will continue to storm the gates. At some point, virtually every organization seeks new markets, new ideas, new suppliers, and broader opportunities.

But if we're going to hunt new business in an unexplored territory, let's at least do it right.

Here are some hard-won lessons on what works and what doesn't when it comes to prospecting.

Where to Start?

Close to home.

High up on your prospecting list should be anyone you have done business with in the past, including former associates who have moved on to new organizations. Other good sources of prospect leads are friends, acquaintances, or people you know from industry, social, or civic associations.

I'm often asked if joining civic, business, or charitable groups will help business. My response is consistent—joining these groups can put you in contact with potential opportunities, *but* don't join purely for the selfish reason of selling more business. Join if you're really interested in the group and their activities and want to play an active role that will include attending meetings and functions. You will meet business and government leaders when you're involved with these groups, but let the business discussions be natural and not forced. Earlier we talked about Intent. We defined Intent as a sincere desire to help clients be successful. Intent carries over into civic, business, and charitable work as well. Join because your Intent is to help. Contacts and opportunities will probably come over time, but you've got to join for the right reasons.

Create the Right Prospect Profile

A personal entrée to a new client is ideal, but for even the best connected professionals, they will take you only so far. At some point, you will want and need to cast a wider net.

Companies similar to existing customers are a natural fit, as are companies with comparable needs or opportunities. For example, if your company sells language translation services, find companies doing business in the countries where you have the most proficiency. If you've had success selling to mid-sized banks, it only makes sense to broaden your sales efforts in that market segment and consider other mid-market financial institutions, such as insurance or capital markets. You've got the references and the know-how; you just need the awareness.

A Time to Strike!

Creating the right prospect profile will help you focus your marketing and selling efforts on the highest potential targets. There are two caveats that demand action.

The first occurs when a prospect you've identified is unhappy with one of your competitors. Perhaps there was a delivery or service issue. Maybe the problem was handled to the customer's satisfaction, or maybe not. If you have created some awareness of your company's services and capabilities through meetings, sales materials, mailings and so forth, you might get a call. Does this happen? Not nearly as often as we'd like, but it does happen. The problem is simple; the sales process is not in your hands, it's in the prospect's hands. However, if you have some limited Mind Share, you just might get the call.

The second condition is in your hands. It's called change. By monitoring the Internet, industry publications, and newspapers, and by networking religiously with business contacts, you can spot significant changes, such as the hiring of a new senior executive. Or perhaps an acquisition is being contemplated or has been completed. There may be a sudden surge or decrease in the prospect's revenue or earnings, or maybe they've introduced a new product or service. Whatever the change is, now is the time to be proactive. Change has occurred, and this may mean who gets the business will be rethought and perhaps restructured.

Following the appointment of a new CEO from another company, you can bet there will be considerable change. A new ad agency—or perhaps a new law firm or auditor may be selected.

So the good news is that "change is in the air." The bad news is that your smart competitors will descend on the prospect in anticipation of possible new business. Therefore, you've got to have a set of messages and an approach that will resonate with your prospect.

Combine UniqueConnect and Solid Messages

You're armed with a list of prospects, including companies with a profile similar to many of your current customers, referrals from business colleagues, and organizations experiencing major change in their business. You've visited their Web sites, called and asked for information packages to review, and done your homework. Now you're ready to go for an appointment. Before you make that first call, let's consider the impact of combining the UniqueConnect strategy and solid messages.

Remember, UniqueConnect is a name, a fact, an idea, or an introduction used to establish a strong and immediate rapport with a prospect. In almost any business, the very best UniqueConnect is a referral or introduction from a mutual friend or associate.

So the opening of that phone call might sound like this:

> "Susan, this is Richard Smith with Vertigo Industries," you begin. Elaine Hansen mentioned that the two of you play tennis regularly. Elaine and I are friends. Your name came up in a conversation the other day, and Elaine suggested I give you a call."

What do you do if you don't have a referral or friend as your UniqueConnect? It's time to review the information we uncovered in our research steps and determine the next, best UniqueConnect. Since you don't have a referral or a friend, the UniqueConnect may be new information or an interesting piece of market research.

Here's what that phone call might sound like:

> "Susan, this is Richard Smith with the Vertigo Industries," you begin. "My company recently published a White Paper based on market research in the oil and gas industry. Since you are a supplier to the energy industry, I thought you might find it interesting. I'll drop it off at your office tomorrow afternoon."

Let's look at another UniqueConnect where you don't have a referral, but one that emphasizes you've done your homework.

> "Susan, this is Richard Smith with Vertigo Industries. From visiting your Web site and reading about your company in a recent travel industry magazine, I quickly learned how important security systems are to your business. That's

the heart of our business, and we've had great success in working with our clients to improve overall security, without adding to headcount."

Straightforward, logical, and, hopefully, productive.

Are these UniqueConnects going to work? Yes, they will work with prospects but not as often as they will with customers. It's simply human nature to make an appointment with someone you have done business with before or with someone highly recommended.

The real point with prospects is to have the confidence that based on your homework and some creative and informed thinking, you have a UniqueConnect.

If you can't do that, don't waste your time (or theirs).

"Treat Customers Like Prospects!"

Think about all that you and your company do to win new business:

- ◆ You do your homework
- ◆ Overcome the jitters and make the appointment
- ◆ Prepare for the call
- ◆ Follow up with information
- ◆ Deliver presentations
- ◆ Create proposals
- ◆ Visit the home office
- ◆ Bring in "the boss"
- ◆ Set up business lunches and entertainment
- ◆ . . . and finally; **THE CONTRACT**

Many sales professionals and companies now assign their newest client a computer-generated customer number and begin treating them like a "customer." Wrong approach; don't do it!

You must continue to treat customers as you would the most valuable prospect the company has. The most obvious reason to keep doing the right thing is that you promised value during the sales process and you've got to deliver on that promise. It also keeps your customer in the position of perhaps providing you with referrals, both internally and externally.

Our Customer . . . Their Prospect!

But there's an even more basic reason. Once a prospect becomes your customer, they become prime prospects for all your competitors. Earlier, we talked about going after "underserved customers" belonging to your competitors. They're vulnerable when they're underserved—and smart salespeople know it!

So the real enemies are complacency, lethargy, "we have a contract" mentality, and lack of new ideas. In other words, your Intent has shifted from making your customer successful to finding new prospects. Any crack in the wall, and in pours the competition—all doing the right things to show your customer the benefits of doing business with their company. Put yourself in your competitor's shoes . . . they have nothing to lose when they go after your customer, so they will pull out all stops.

What's the message? Keep doing the things that got you the business in the first place. Delivering insightful information, building relationships wide and deep, bringing in experts to help, following up quickly, checking on service and value consistently. Keep your Intent to help them be successful front and center.

Treat all customers like prospects and don't take them for granted!

SUMMARY

◆ Prospects and clients are bombarded by salespeople wanting to save them time and money. Therefore, it's very hard to see them without a UniqueConnect.

◆ The strongest UniqueConnect is a mutual business and/ or personal friend. This means that networking with people from the industry is critical.

◆ Generally, the second best UniqueConnect is valuable Information. But you must put the Information to the test. Is it really valuable and potentially useful?

◆ Other UniqueConnects must be stated logically and clearly in order to break through the other "sales clutter" most decision makers hear and see daily. In other words, there must be perceived value in meeting with you.

◆ Keep treating customers as prospects. Continue to do the things that got the business in the first place. If you don't, your competitors will!

◆ Following an intial call, write a letter summarizing the Key Points you discussed. Make sure you briefly describe how you might be able to help. Read the letter carefully. If it makes sense, send it. If it doesn't, ask yourself if you really have a prospect!

Chapter

THE TOOL KIT

To this point we've emphasized I^3 . . . Intent, Information, and Insight. We then introduced the UniqueConnect concept. Based on the UniqueConnect model, we put heavy emphasis on protecting and growing our most valuable customers. The next highest priority is prospecting for new business by leveraging a UniqueConnect whenever possible.

With I^3 and UniqueConnect as the guiding principles for our business development efforts, it's appropriate to open our Tool Kit and consider ten, time-tested ideas to further accelerate your selling efforts.

"How Come I Don't Have That in My Tool Kit?"

Watch an experienced handyman doing some work around your home. Some of the work is fairly simple and gets handled in a flash. Other jobs require experience, a clear sense of the options, and The Tool Kit. You and I might go to the local hardware store and buy a tool kit, but it will be a far cry from the one an experienced handyman uses. Special pliers here, some bent wire there, a couple of items that almost defy description . . . all tools that get the job done!

The same thing applies to your Sales Tool Kit. Years of selling and working with sales professionals has convinced me that these tools will make a difference before and after the sales cycle. They are tools that work. They may have to be modified for your products or services, or they may need a little tweaking to reflect how you sell and the industries you call on. Take a look at each and apply the ones that will work best for you. It's now your Sales Tool Kit!

TOOL #1: KEY MESSAGES

A Runaway Elevator Speech

The Information Week 500 Conference at Hilton Head Island was almost over. It had been three days of working the booth, listening to speeches, and schmoozing with clients and prospects. I was tired, but anxious to pack and head for the airport.

I got on the elevator, and just as the doors started to close, Paul Allaire, the CEO of Xerox and the keynote speaker for the conference, entered the elevator. I told him I enjoyed his speech. He thanked me and politely asked, "So, what is Andersen Consulting (now named Accenture) up to these days?"

What a perfect opening! I was in the middle of the famous forty-five-second elevator speech and didn't even know it!

Here, word for word, was my response:

> "Well, Mr. Allaire, we're staying busy, that's for sure. How 'bout Xerox?"

He agreed that the good folks at Xerox were also busy. He smiled. This was child's play for him. I was no challenge. No reason to sound the horn and bring in Andersen Consulting so far. I tossed him a few more verbal softballs.

Why couldn't we start this ride over at the ground floor? I just knew I could win him over! But alas, a few more equally dynamic comments back and forth, and he got off the elevator. I did tell him one more time that I enjoyed his speech. He nodded and smiled that smooth CEO grin . . . my chance for breaking down the door had evaporated!

Is There Really an Elevator Speech?

I wish we all had regular chance meetings with CEOs of Fortune 500 companies while taking a forty-five-second elevator ride. Such is not life and also not the purpose of the elevator speech.

The elevator speech is a vivid way to suggest that you should be able to communicate a couple of hard-hitting, memorable messages in a short period of time. That's true whether in an elevator, on an airplane, or walking into the office of someone you've wanted to meet for months.

So what's memorable? "One if by land, two if by sea!" I'd call that memorable and done in a lot less than forty-five seconds! And perhaps, "Where did that iceberg come from?" also qualifies. But these are historical moments. Where are the business examples?

In the Beginning . . .

To start creating solid Key Messages, you might review some of the ads your company has run, look at the Web site, and read present and past brochures and proposals. By examining the key points being made, you will have a sense of what your organization is trying to tell its customers, prospects, employees, and vendors—all of its audiences.

Key Messages are designed to differentiate your company from the competition and give the buyer a set of reasons to consider your offerings. The themes for most Key Messages center on these areas:

◆ Credentials such as size, locations, number of employees, length of time in business, unique services, and skill sets.

- How you perform the work that you do, and the results for your users.

- Specific case studies or examples of "before and after" results.

- Customer reference lists.

- Provocative statements or questions designed to get a response such as, "I'd like more information on that."

- Information about new services or products that are "better, faster, cheaper."

- Points about innovation, total cost of ownership, and customer service.

- Ways to answer the question, "How are you different?"

Nice "corporate messages" but you've got to personalize them for specific sales opportunities. Here are the guidelines to follow:

Introducing Proof Points

At the opening of virtually any meeting, there will be introductions and an exchange of pleasantries, after which it's time to provide a quick introduction about the purpose of the meeting. We call this "stage setting."

You'll want to have a few well-crafted messages that are almost committed to memory but don't sound memorized. To ensure a smooth and complete delivery of the Key Messages, I recommend you have just a couple of "trigger words" on your note-taking page to guide this important conversation. Examples might include the UniqueConnect, the name of a new study you've read, or a point you saw in an industry write-up.

Your key points should be crafted to help you:

- ◆ Establish initial rapport.
- ◆ Gain interest quickly.
- ◆ *Briefly* position your company and solutions.

Always Support the Key Message with Something That Anchors It in the Mind of the Listener.

When you deliver a Key Message, it's important to anchor it with an example or a Proof Point to give it credibility. A Proof Point is specific measurable information such as "25 percent increase in profits," or "finishing the job in two weeks instead of four weeks." For example, stating that your company serves the global market is interesting but bland unless your potential competitors are unable to make the same statement. By adding a Proof Point, you speak to the degree and depth of the global presence your company enjoys.

So the statement might sound like this: "We serve the global market. In fact, over 40 percent of our revenue last year came from outside the USA. I've also plotted your locations and with one exception, we have offices in each of those countries." Now we've added quantifiable information to our Key Message and personalized it for the prospect.

Here's another example: "We're a very innovative company." This is a Key Message; however it lacks specifics. Taking it to the extreme, what competitor would state, "We're not innovative"?

The Key Message about innovation could be anchored by stating, "We'd like to think we're very innovative in our approach to product development. In fact, last year we spent over 15 percent of revenue in pure research and development. An example of the payoff from that type of investment is the fact that we were granted twenty patents last year."

Here are examples connecting Themes, Key Messages, and Proof Points:

Themes →	Key Messages →	Proof Points
Reduced Risk →	Our staff has deep skills and industry knowledge. →	The average project manager has 15+ years in the business and has managed at least 10 similar projects.
Efficiency and Productivity →	Research from three industry analysts suggests dramatic production increases with our systems. →	The minimal gain in manufacturing and engineering productivity was 20 percent over two years.
Effective Training →	We provide on-site training, e-learning, and 1-800-URCOACH. →	A decrease of 33 percent in error rates is typical in a major factory installation.
Flexible Pricing →	Our clients can choose between a fixed price contract or a per transaction price. →	Whatever pricing model you choose, the contract provides annual comparisons for each type of pricing and allows for renegotiation to another plan.

By using examples such as these on the chart, the Key Messages are strengthened and given dimension. Hopefully, our prospect will value and remember our Key Messages, and will communicate them to the other decision makers in the organization. Why is that important? Because someone who has not attended your meeting may ask your contact, "What does that company bring to the table?" Your contact's response will either propel your company forward or put you right in the middle of the pack . . . not an enviable position.

Understand your company's Key Messages, and if they're not anchored with Proof Points develop your own. Prospects buy because they can see the problem answered or the opportunity realized. The more proof we can provide, the more memorable our Key Messages will be, thereby distinguishing them from fuzzy corporate-speak.

A Second Chance with the Xerox CEO

Remember my weak attempt at an elevator speech with Paul Allaire, CEO of Xerox? Well, since I'm the author of this book, I'm going to give myself another chance.

"So, what is Andersen Consulting up to these days?" asks Mr. Allaire.

"Thank you for asking, Mr. Allaire. As a matter of fact, the demand for installation of major software systems is really keeping us busy. How is your business?" I respond.

"It's certainly challenging and keeps us busy as well," he answers.

"I'll bet it does. With your busy schedule and speaking at events such as this conference, how do you stay connected to the office?" I ask.

"It's tough, but we use our voice mail and conference calls to keep up when we're on the road [note, e-mail was not in widespread use in 1995]," replies Mr. Allaire.

"Several of our clients have had the same challenge. Working together, we've developed a new approach and the results have been impressive. Whom do you suggest I call on your staff?" I quiz.

"Give Pat Tolan a call and let her know I asked you to," he responds.

"Thank you, I will. And again, I enjoyed your speech today," I conclude.

"Thanks. Have a safe trip home."

Unfortunately, I didn't get the second chance to tell Mr. Allaire about the new communication tool. If I had had a second opportunity the conversation would have gone much better as I would have used some Key Messages and kept them brief.

The next chart describes a five-step process to develop messages that gain interest. Each step is short, makes clear measurable points, and demonstrates the value of your products and services.

Key Sales Messages in Practice
This is a five-step process designed to gain interest.

Describe a current market condition.
"The paper industry has shown greatly-improved overall earnings but often has capacity problems, except in High Performance Mills."

Cite a specific opportunity.
"HPM is a high-performance mill delivering sustainable results."

Present evidence.
"HPM has consistent profit margins of 5 percent. This compares to the industry average of 2 to 3 percent profit margins."

Position your company as the best choice.
"We've worked closely with HPM and two of the three largest forest products companies to achieve and sustain these results."

Deliver a unique and compelling message.
"By investing now, you will be able to maximize production to allow for market demand and volume increases and still preserve the higher profit margins."

SUMMARY

◆ Avoid generalizations such as, "We're global," or, "We believe in customer service."

◆ Anchor each message with at least one Proof Point that can be measured. "We were able to increase output 10 percent," or, "There was an overall savings of 15 percent."

◆ Key messages are short and hopefully memorable. "The revised compensation plan reduced key employee turnover by 20 percent."

◆ Keep the Key Messages fresh and current by constantly updating and revising them to reflect market conditions.

◆ All communications (written, verbal, Internet, marketing materials, etc.) must reinforce the Key Messages . . . It builds the brand and gains Mind Share.

◆ Key Messages can help you answer two tough questions: "So what?" and "How are you different?"

TOOL #2: VOICE MAIL

"Hi, this is Mike Simmons. I'm away from my desk right now, so please leave a detailed message and I'll call you right back."

Don't Bet on It!

The world is flooded with voice mail, e-mail, and regular mail. Unless a businessperson is absolutely fascinated by the first words out of your mouth, they'll hit the erase button . . . and you're history. In fact, research and common sense tell us that as few as 10 percent of the prospects you call will return a "cold call" voice mail.

But people do return *certain* voice mail messages. In fact, if you employ some logic and straight thinking, your callback rate will be as much as 30 percent higher.

The simple fact is this: voice mail can and does work for many successful salespeople.

Here's how to make it work for you.

Learn the Basics of Persistence

How many times should you call and leave a voice mail? Professionals who set appointments for a living suggest calling up to seven times. That seems like a lot, but it works. Their experience shows that your "hit rate" will improve after four or five calls. Perhaps it's because the prospect now realizes you're serious about the call. However, while persistence can pay off, it's still a numbers game with a low probability of success unless you carefully craft short, high-impact voice mail messages and use a UniqueConnect.

Using the Power of UniqueConnect

To get your foot in the "telephone door," leverage the power of the UniqueConnect. Refer to the chapter on UniqueConnects, how to use them, and how to create a UniqueConnect if you don't already have one.

When leaving a voice mail message, you should be able to state your UniqueConnect in fewer than fifteen seconds. If you don't have a UniqueConnect, leaving a voice mail may not be worth your time. So, the key is a UniqueConnect and a brief message.

Short and Sweet

How long should a voice mail be? No longer than *thirty seconds,* and less if possible. You should write out your voice mail message first. Time it. Practice it. Revise it. A winning voice mail will consist of the following:

◆ A quick introduction—your name and your company (six to eight seconds).

◆ Your UniqueConnect (twelve to fifteen seconds).

◆ A clear, time-referenced call to action and a phone number (eight to ten seconds).

Here's how it might sound:

"This is Sue Jones with The Allen Group. Bill Evans suggested I call you. We've been able to reduce his inventory costs by 16 percent and Bill thought you would be interested in our approach. I'll call you Thursday at 2 p.m. to set an appointment. My number is 970-555-1246. I look forward to talking with you."

That, for my money, is an effective voice mail. First, we have a UniqueConnect—Bill Evans. Second, there is a clear "value message"—reduce inventory costs by 16 percent. It concludes with a specific follow-up plan.

So let's break down the thirty seconds into three groups. As scenarios 1 and 2 show, we have one example of a voice mail where we have a reference and one where we don't, but instead have a solid piece of information. Notice how one main theme—or UniqueConnect—is used for each. In addition, there is a clear course of action.

SCENARIO 1: Referral from a mutual friend.

Opening	UniqueConnect	Action Step
Hi. This is Bob Logan with the Forest Company.	Tom Hogan and I have worked together on several projects for his company. He suggested that I contact you.	I'll call you Tuesday afternoon to see when we can get together. Again, my name is Bob Logan and my phone number is 215-555-4344. I look forward to talking with you on Tuesday.
3 seconds	*8 seconds*	*14 seconds*

Total voice mail time = 25 seconds.

| OPENING | UNIQUECONNECT | ACTION STEP |

SCENARIO 2: Information that may be important to the prospect.

Opening	**UniqueConnect**	**Action Step**
Hi. This is Bob Logan with the Forest Company.	Recently I attended an industry conference and met several of your customers. Based on those meetings, I think we may have something of interest for you.	I'll call you Tuesday afternoon to arrange a brief meeting. Again, my name is Bob Logan and my phone number is 215-555-4344. I look forward to talking with you on Tuesday.
3 seconds	*10 seconds*	*14 seconds*

Total voice mail time = 27 seconds.

Practice Makes Perfect

How good is your voice mail message? Unfortunately, prospects don't complete a J. D. Powers survey on your voice mails and give you feedback. But here's a very practical and timesaving way to find out how good your voice mail messages are.

When you get home tonight, call your own number and leave your voice mail message. Then tomorrow morning, listen to the message with a critical ear. Is your voice mail clear, concise, and compelling? Ask a colleague or two to critique your voice mail, and listen to their input with an open mind.

Successful salespeople constantly assess and refine their sales messages for face-to-face meetings. Apply that principle to your voice mail efforts.

If you manage a sales organization, you can use this same approach on a larger scale.

Let's Work on It Together: The Power of Group Thinking!

At your next sales meeting, describe a basic sales situation to your group. Ask them to record a voice mail message on their own office phone, trying to get an appointment. Then get together and review the messages. Do this in the spirit of collaboration; in other words, in a positive way. After everyone has had a chance to hear their messages and get some feedback, take this opportunity to review the basics of good voice mail messaging. Take the best thinking from the group and develop two to three voice mail templates everyone can use. Just make sure they don't "get old" by revisiting them on a regular basis, perhaps quarterly, and updating them.

Here's a Final Tip

When you get an appointment, ask your prospect how you came across on voice mail and what he or she thinks is the best approach to getting a return phone call. You'll be amazed at their willingness to give you very helpful input. Remember, your prospects are probably struggling with how to leave great voice mails themselves!

SUMMARY

◆ The odds are not in your favor in getting a return call after leaving a voice mail, but using a UniqueConnect can dramatically improve the odds.

◆ Effective voice mails are short . . . less than thirty seconds!

◆ Only deliver one Key Message in a voice mail.

◆ Be persistent and follow up several times, but try to vary the voice mail message so that it isn't the "same old thing" each time.

◆ Talk slowly, and if you leave your number, say it twice. Nothing is harder than trying to write down ten numbers you haven't heard before, particularly if the person talks fast.

◆ Keep a log on returned e-mails and voice mails to see which is most effective and if there are any trends on which you can capitalize. For example, you may find that executives respond more often to e-mails—or you may discover that mid-level managers tend to call back after a voice mail.

TOOL #3: IDEAS ON GETTING IN

At the beginning of the book, I stated that my purpose in writing *Boardroom Selling* was *not* to recreate another sales methodology. Hopefully I'm accomplishing the real objective and that is to share my thoughts and experiences in selling. You can then pick and choose what works best for you.

As an active public speaker on the subject of sales, I'm frequently asked about techniques for "Getting In" to see a prospect. As you know by now, I do not subscribe to the thinking that selling is about Cold Calling and "Getting In" when they don't want to see you in the first place!

However, keep in mind that you, the reader, are my client, and that my Intent is to help you succeed. Here are three techniques that have worked well for me.

Calling on the Assistant

The larger the organization, and the higher you go, the more likely you are to encounter an executive assistant.

First, you must have a clear understanding of the role of executive assistants. Their job is to ensure that the executive sees the people they should see . . . and is not bothered by the people they should not see. In addition, they work closely together with the decision maker on projects, schedules, and travel. Enormous trust in each other is almost a given, and the input from the assistant is listened to . . . carefully.

Changing the Game

Most assistants are very adept in the art of "getting you off the phone." They're usually very polite, but firm. They may suggest you talk with someone else, generally someone much lower in the pecking order. Or they may simply share the fact with you that the executive "doesn't see salespeople." Other obstacles include travel schedules and simply, "not available."

Can you get appointments by working through the assistant? Your chances increase considerably if you have a UniqueConnect such as a mutual friend. But without a strong UniqueConnect, let's face it: cold phone calls to set up appointments are hard and often end in rejection.

There's a better way, but it requires the investment in *two calls* to get to see the executive.

The first call is on the assistant *but not on the phone*. You are going to drop in at his or her office and ask to talk to the assistant, *not the executive*. Here's the logic. Assistants are not used to being called on in person. The exception may be someone from the coffee service or the travel agency. They are prepared to deal with phone calls, but become different people when the receptionist tells them they have a guest in the lobby.

Curiosity usually takes over and they come out to meet you. Occasionally, the receptionist has handed me the phone. If that happens, I introduce myself and state that I made it a point to come by and meet them and ask if they have a moment. It usually works, and an assistant will venture out "for just a moment."

What Do You Say?

First of all, you're making a call on a professional, so act like one. You're not doing the executive assistant a favor and you certainly don't outrank them! Smile, offer to shake hands, introduce yourself, and provide a business card. The dialogue that has been most effective for me sounds like this:

"I always do a lot of research on the companies I want to earn the right to do business with [key phrase]. I'm sure your senior salespeople do the same. Your boss's name kept coming up as I was doing my homework as someone I should meet. I would like to introduce myself to Mr. Hammond and he can quickly determine if my services would be of benefit. The meeting can be as short as fifteen minutes. Do you normally schedule that type of meeting?" Another genuine smile, stop talking, and let the assistant respond.

I've had very good success with this approach and recommend it highly. One guideline—don't attempt to overpower the assistant or intimidate. It won't work.

Sell yourself to the assistant, and you are halfway to the executive. Imagine the impact when you come in for the appointment and the assistant greets you with, "Nice to see you again, come on in!" Oh, one more important point. Don't automatically assume the decision maker is male and the executive assistant is female. It simply doesn't work that way in the real world.

Action Letters

One way to get your message in front of a potential prospect is to send what I call an Action Letter.

This message can be sent via e-mail, in a FedEx package, or via traditional post. Think of it as a "supercharged direct mail piece," because it is precisely targeted, includes a UniqueConnect, and delivers a salient message to your prospect.

Sample Letter:

(Date)

Carol Watkins, Senior Vice President
Myers-Adams Labs
43210 Main Street
New York, NY 10017

Dear Carol:

Over the past eighteen months, my company has worked closely with Tim Higgins of HFW Pharmaceutical on a "speed to market" initiative. I'm aware that you attend industry group meetings with Tim. We have been able to deliver significant results to HFW including:

◆ Reduction in new product returns of almost 22 percent.

◆ Inventory reductions equalling $12 million in annual savings.

◆ Order rate increases averaging 25 percent.

The system and process we use aggregates ordering data from the pharmacies, compares the new data to established ordering histories, and projects sales volumes accordingly. The end result is fewer out-of-stock conditions, faster inventory turns, and better market data.

Tim suggested I summarize our results to date and contact you. Hopefully this brief overview of the "hard numbers" is both helpful and intriguing. I'll call your office Friday at 11:00 a.m. to see when we might schedule a meeting. Thank you in advance.

Sincerely,
Dennis Reynolds

As you read the letter, notice the keen Insight into the prospect's company, the industry, and the business challenges they face. The idea is to garner interest from the reader because the Information is hard hitting and on target.

As the letter suggests, you will be following up at a set time. "I'll call your office next week," simply doesn't cut it. You certainly wouldn't schedule a meeting for "sometime next week," would you? When is "sometime next week" anyway? Be specific with date and time. I've actually had assistants tell me, "He or she was expecting your call!"

Let's Push the Envelope a Little

Want to play for slightly higher stakes? Try this idea. Send the action letter to your primary target and copy his or her boss. Your prospect has to make a decision: bring you in for a meeting, or risk having the boss ask what they thought of the ideas outlined in the letter. This is a particularly aggressive approach, and may not be appropriate for every prospect.

Whether or not you copy people on the letter is your call. But Action Letters with disciplined follow-up work well. My advice is to use them selectively and make sure they have real impact. When you talk to someone who has received the letter, ask his or her opinion of its effectiveness and make modifications accordingly.

Who Else Has Been There?

Here's one more prospecting idea that I stumbled on when I was making a call on a new prospect.

Most companies maintain sign-in books at the receptionist's

desk. Visitors sign in and print their name and that of the company, time, date, and the person they are seeing. We all know the drill and have been through it hundreds of times. That's the problem. We sign in and rarely take advantage of the information on the sign-in sheet. It can be of tremendous value to you.

As you look at the sign-in sheet, you may see the names of people in the company you would like to meet. Make a note of the salesperson and company that called on them. Then assuming they are not direct competitors, it might be worth your while

DATE	NAME	COMPANY	VISITING	TIME IN	TIME OUT
7/1	B. Morris	Elk Shelving	B. Hayden	8:30	9:30
7/1	Alice Decker	Self	Mike Connors	11:00	12:15
7/1	Ken Tucker	Ohio Plumbing	Kelly Kornan	11:15	12:45
7/1	AF Farraday	Simmons Co.	Darwin	1:30	2:00
7/1	Christy	AllFlip Coffee	Dawson	1:45	3:30

to give that person a call.

Taking our lead from the sign-in sheet, we want to call Ken Tucker since he called on the person we wanted to meet, Kelly Kornan.

"Hey Ken, this is Steve Carson with EFT Corporation," you might say. "I noticed you were at Ohio Plumbing the other day calling on Kelly Kornan. I've been trying to see her forever, and since we don't compete, I was wondering if I could buy you a cup of coffee and see what magic you spun to get in there?"

"And by the way, if there is someplace you have been trying to get in where I'm doing business, I'd be more than happy to return the favor."

Be polite but forthright, and don't be afraid to enlist the help of your fellow road warriors.

As you know, I don't like cold calls. I like UniqueConnect selling. These three techniques can help in your prospecting endeavors since they do use some of the concepts of UniqueConnect.

SUMMARY

◆ Treat the Executive Assistant (EA) with respect . . . it's important to have relationships with both the executive and the trusted assistant.

◆ After a meeting with an EA, send a short note or e-mail and try to work in something personal if possible. "Did your son's team win the game on Saturday?" or, "Did you enjoy the trip to San Francisco as much as you thought you would?" or, "Thanks for working me into the schedule last Wednesday; I know it was hectic with the staff meeting on the same day."

◆ Keep prospecting letters to one page . . . take the time to write a short letter!

◆ Break out of the clutter by including compelling statistics, results, and metrics in the letter. Avoid "glittering generalities" and show the recipient you've done your homework.

◆ Try making a "sales call" on the EA . . . it works!

◆ Call on a salesperson who was able to meet with the person you're interested in seeing.

TOOL #4: DIRECT MAIL WITH A DIFFERENCE

Here's a question that gets asked during sales workshops, following a speech, or when I'm out making sales calls with a client's sales team.

"Does Direct Mail Really Work?"

The consultant's answer is "It depends." Unfortunately, the real-world answer to that question is the same. It really does depend on a number of factors. I'll list them first and then give you an approach that does result in appointments by combining our UniqueConnect strategy and good direct mail technique. First, the key factors for success in any direct mail program are:

- ◆ Good material—It must be interesting, to the point, provocative, enlightening, and easy to understand.

- ◆ Quality mailing list—The program is doomed for failure without a good list of names, and correct titles and addresses.

- ◆ Strong follow-up—Mailings must have disciplined follow-up. A very clever direct mail piece asking the recipient to respond might work, but I've seen very few that qualify.

With these guidelines in place, we're ready to launch our mailing program. My best success has come from a two-part mailing strategy. I find that spacing the mailings about five to seven working days apart keeps continuity and is not overwhelming from an administrative perspective.

What Should We Mail?

Good question, and it's one best left to your marketing people and the direct mail experts. I've seen many different types of effective mailings over the years such as:

◆ An oversized aspirin tablet (I mean large, like four to five inches across!) with a simple note saying, "If you have headaches with your phone system, take one of these or call me!" A business card was enclosed.

◆ A small clock neatly packed in a red mailing tube. The card simply read, "It's time to get together; I've got a great idea for you!" A business card was enclosed.

◆ A binder with the results of a recent study of consumer spending habits mailed to selected retailers. The note indicated the date the recipient would be contacted.

◆ A small box containing a sand dollar from the beach. The card stated, "Some dollars you can find on the beach; others come from our kind of insight into your benefit plans!" A date was given for a follow-up phone call from the company.

◆ A cartoon in the form of a poster was placed in a mailing tube with a card suggesting there were more cartoons available and the phone number to call. The cartoons depicted common business situations and rivaled the Garfield the cat series. This was very well received.

◆ Buy reprints of industry articles and then prepare a Point of View (POV) in reference to the article. Be sure your POV displays solid thinking or even a differing opinion. Make it provocative if possible. Mail the article with your POV and follow up with a call. It's an inexpensive way to put useful information in decision makers' hands.

Direct Mail Guidelines

◆ Unless you are in the business of making and selling "homemade items"; quality wins in direct mail. Resist the temptation to "do it on the cheap". Your results will be in direct proportion to the creativity, relevance, and quality of the elements of the program.

◆ Forget your favorite direct mail pieces; it's interesting, but not terribly important. Map your choices to your audience, not to your personal choices (or those of the boss either!). You may like humor, but does your audience? Cajun themes may work in New Orleans, but what about your east coast audiences? Wildly creative — or — conservative; keep the audience in mind.

◆ Less is more . . . avoid the desire to write an editorial with tons of copy Use more graphically compelling approaches and fewer words. The goal is to create interest, not tell your whole story in the mailing.

◆ Re-enforce corporate and product Key Messages in the copy, but pick one or two of the Messages at most — "brevity is the soul of wit" according to Shakespeare . . . and it applies to direct mail as well.

◆ Assume that your mailing will probably receive rough handling at the post office or by the shipper and package accordingly.

◆ The second most important aspect of the program is strong follow-up. Allow sufficient time to follow-up quickly and for the increase in meetings that will result.

Making the Program Different and Effective

By adding two simple steps, you will see greatly improved results in your direct mail program. Response rates should move from single digits into the 15 to 20 percent range.

1. Buy the best mailing list possible and add your clients and prospects to it.

2. Select or create two excellent mailers and agree on the number you plan to send. I suggest five mailings at a time due to the follow-up required by the program.

3. Here's the new "twist"! Call to get the correct spelling of the recipient's name, title, and address. You'd be surprised how many people have a nickname or initials that don't show up on the mailing list. It may be Bill Jones that's preferred, not R. William Jones. Then, finish the call by saying, "I'm going to be sending something to Bill later this week, and I would appreciate it if you could make sure he gets it. Thanks!"

4. Send the first round of mailers and enter the information into your database.

5. More "good stuff"! Between the first and the second mailing (usually five to seven days apart), call a **second time.** This call is to advise that a second mailing is coming. Don't ask if the first mailing was received. Calling the second time is new and rarely done in conventional, direct-mail programs. This technique can spell the difference between a ho-hum program and one that breaks new ground!

6. Send the second mailer and follow up.

7. Update your database.

Steps to Take for an Effective Direct Mail Program

1

Mailing List

Mailing List
- ◆ Buy/create list
- ◆ Decide how many to mail each week
- ◆ Enter information into database

2

Mailers

Develop Creative Mailers
- ◆ Select both mailers
- ◆ Make them distinctive, e.g., a red envelope

3

Info Call

Call for Information/To Advise
- ◆ Call for correct name, title, address
- ◆ Advise assistant "the mailer is coming!"
- ◆ Enter assistant's name in database

4

Send Mailer

Send First Mailer
- ◆ Enter date in database
- ◆ Decide on follow-up call date

5

Advise Call

Call to Advise Second Mailer
- ◆ Call assistant to advise—second mailing is coming
- ◆ Subtly find out if first mailing was received
- ◆ Thank assistant for help

6

Send Mailer

Send Second Mailer
- ◆ Enter date in database
- ◆ Decide on follow-up call date

7

Follow Up

Strong Follow Up
- ◆ Call on exact date selected
- ◆ Don't ask if they received mailers
- ◆ Assume they did and ask for an appointment
- ◆ Enter results in database

Now you know why I strongly suggest you do no more than five mailings each week. We are not mass mailing in this program. We are UniqueConnect mailing by adding the critical steps three and five. Of course the program falls apart unless you stay the course. Do it by the numbers and follow up when you say you will. Soon you'll be setting up appointments and not just licking a lot of stamps and hoping for positive responses.

SUMMARY

◆ Targeted direct mail requires more work, such as:

-Carefully selecting quality material that is also creative,

-Placing a call to get the right name, title, and address, and

-Advising the recipient of each mailing and informing them "It is coming!"

◆ The program will fail or produce weak results without strong follow up.

◆ Avoid "mailing the world" unless you are in the mass-marketing business.

◆ Keep accurate, updated records (Customer Relationship Management [CRM] or other system) to measure results.

TOOL #5: ASKING GREAT QUESTIONS

Years ago when I was an IBM branch manager, I was heading out to make a day of calls with one of my salespeople. We were to visit a large industrial glass company in Toledo, Ohio. As we drove up, I asked my associate what he planned to do on the call.

"Oh, we'll play it by ear," he said. That was not what I had in mind.

"Hold on," I responded. "This is a major customer. Instead of playing it by ear, let's be creative."

I proposed that when we walked into our customer's office, something unexpected would happen. Our customer would suddenly announce that due to budget constraints, all questions from vendors would come with a price tag of five dollars each! To further compound this startling development, we had just twenty dollars in our wallets!

The Five-Dollar Question

So what questions should we ask, given the new ground rules? Remember, we're now on a tight budget, and we've got to make each question count.

Since I was the sales manager, I got my way. We sat in the car and came up with four questions specifically crafted to help us understand some of our customer's major business issues. We also wanted to find out what role their department played in solving some of the business issues the company was facing. Finally, we wanted to determine, with their help, how we might move forward in presenting some solutions to the challenges the company was facing.

As I remember it, we used three of the questions we had selected and were able to elicit some very useful information from our contact. Were we successful because we asked the five-dollar questions? That's not the point. The approach made us focus more clearly on the key issues at hand. It worked, and it's a technique I've used throughout my career.

Remember to watch your budget . . . you've only got twenty dollars and the questions cost five dollars each!

Asking the Right Questions

What makes a question worth five dollars if you only have twenty dollars in your wallet?

Remember, at this point we are trying to move the relationship through a series of screens, or filters, which will give us Insight into the prospect's challenges and opportunities. Most five-dollar questions fall into the five categories suggested in the PRIDE chart:

To Gain Valuable Insight, Try Some of the Questions in the PRIDE Model

Personal
How did you decide to come to work here?
Before you started here, where were you working?
How have your responsibilities changed over the past couple of years?
What activities do you enjoy outside of work?

Role in the Organization
How do you see your role on projects such as the one we're discussing?
As decisions involving new investments or projects are being considered, how are you and your staff involved?
How can we best support your business objectives?
Based on experience, who else will be involved in the decision-making process?

Insight
As you look back on the past twelve months, what are you most proud of from a business perspective?
As you look at companies in your industry and outside the industry, who's "getting it right"? What leads you to that conclusion?
What trends in the business do you most closely watch? Why?
If there were one thing you wished had gone better last year, what is it?

Determining Needs
What are the major challenges and opportunities this year?
Whom do you most fear entering your market? Why?
What new market segments are you looking at?
What kinds of cost-reduction efforts are underway?
What customer service initiatives are important this year?

Execution
What is the decision cycle for the work we've been discussing?
How do you construct a business case or ROI?
How will you measure the success of this decision?
How can I earn the right to do business with you and your company?

Personal. Many questions will focus on the current and past performance of your client's or prospect's organization or business unit and that's important. Others will help you get to know the person better and build a strong relationship. Understand their backgrounds, current responsibilities, and outside activities; all form the base for the relationship.

Role in the Organization. You also want to know how your prospect's organization works and the specific role he or she plays. How has that role changed over the past year? How will it change going forward?

How does the company typically makes these kinds of decisions. Who gets involved? What's the process? What are the critical points considered in evaluating the business case and the ROI?

Ask about the culture and expectations. How does the prospect interact with other internal groups which may be affected by your solution? How does the prospect measure the satisfaction of those internal clients? What metrics are tracked most closely? Can a senior manager approve a contract or does it take a committee or someone else? Who has ultimate authority?

Insight. At some point during the discussion, your questions should focus on the prospect's view of the world and the future.

What does the prospect expect to see in the economy and in the marketplace? Will the company launch any new initiatives, and if so, when? Does the prospect foresee new competitive pressures? If your homework has given you some Insight into the prospect's situation, use that knowledge as a starting point from which to get into the details. Mention an industry report and ask for your prospect's thoughts and perceptions.

Determining Needs. Being a good salesperson is a bit like being a good talk show host. Learn to ask intelligent, open questions, then sit back and listen. The theory of Need Satisfaction Selling is to determine the prospect's needs and then fill them. Sounds simple, doesn't it? Well, it's not. It takes great questions and strong listening skills. The tendency is to ask one or two questions, get the answer, and then "dive to your solution or product." Resist the temptation to show what you and your company can do. Ask a few more penetrating questions first.

When you ask questions to get at the needs of an organization, it's important to really understand what is being said, and to tap into the evidence that the need is real, measurable, and impacts the organization. Examples of effective follow-up questions are:

◆ How do you measure that?

◆ What have you tried before to solve that issue?

◆ If we could fix that problem of responding more quickly to customer inquiries, what would that enable you to do?

◆ Who in the marketplace is getting it right with regard to the situation we've been talking about?

Execution. A subtle, but very effective technique is to assume that a decision will be made on the need you've identified. The next step is to ask questions about execution and success. The dialogue might go like this: "Let's assume that we're successful in convincing management that a new system makes sense. Based on your experience in similar projects of this magnitude, how will senior management measure success?"

Another approach is to ask how the organization constructs its ROI models or builds a business case for action. Use an example of a past project or purchase to gain Insight into how they will evaluate the investment.

Finally, a great question is to simply ask, "If you could make the decision tomorrow, would we get the business?" Obviously, this is not a question you ask on the first call!

However, it's a great question that could help you find out where you are in the sales process. Knowing where you stand can also help you craft a better plan of action–or to realize that you may not have a qualified prospect.

It's All a Matter of Style

Listen to the conversation at a social event, a cocktail party for example. People are generally standing or sitting around in small groups, talking to each other. Some of the subjects are light and casual; others can be downright stimulating. There are even some business discussions going on and they sound *very different* from the dialogue on many of the sales calls I've witnessed.

If people begin to dominate the conversation with a commercial message about themselves or their companies and products, watch as the listeners find reasons to move away from the "sales pitch." I've found reasons to get another drink or say hello to someone, just to get away from the person who doesn't interact or seem interested in me. I'm sure you have as well!

Why we don't carry the elements of good conversation into a sales call, I don't know. What I do know is we should **interact, not interrogate;** discuss and ask for opinions, not lecture. Have a genuine interest in the other person, and not jump in as soon as there is an opportunity to work in a commercial for our products or services.

Bottom line . . . it's called conversation, not a series of self-serving questions for you, the salesperson, to begin a "verbal PowerPoint presentation."

SUMMARY

◆ Ask a question and then pull the zipper over your lips! I have seen countless great questions asked, only for the salesperson to ramble on and on trying to clarify the question before letting the prospect answer it.

◆ Give them time to answer. They may have to think about the question. Be courteous and wait for them to speak. They'll tell you if they don't want to answer or don't understand the question.

◆ Avoid the temptation to jump in with a product or service as soon as they answer a question. Reflect on the answer, ask another question or two to get more Insight, and review what you heard to gain further agreement. But don't stop asking questions unless the prospect pulls out a pen and insists on signing a contract. In that case, you simply say, "thank you!"

◆ Ask the questions *conversationally*. You are not with the FBI or the IRS, so talk about the issues, but not like it's a jury trial or an inquest!

◆ Short questions are best . . . and they usually get longer answers.

◆ Listen actively. Nod, take a note. Say things like, "I see," "Interesting," "Tell me more." Ask questions like, "What else?" "How did that work out?" "What would you do differently next time?" Smile and act like you've done this before and like to do it!

◆ At the beginning of the meeting tell the prospect why you are asking the questions and what you hope to do with the Information and Insight. Take the mystery out of the equation. "In order to see if we can be of service, I'd like to ask a couple of questions. Is that OK?"

Final thought . . . at five dollars per question, we need to ask the right ones.

TOOL #6: SOLUTION MAPPING

The principle of Solution Mapping is based on two solid pieces of logic. First, the higher you go in an organization, the more you need to focus on Business Drivers, which are the problems and opportunities the decision makers and the company face. You need to figure out how you can address them. *Boardroom Selling* is all about the business issues senior management faces and the value you and your company can bring to help.

Valuable input will come from client and prospect discussions concerning business drivers and your ability to help them work through the issues. Be prepared for lively discussion and even skepticism around "how do we know that will work?" questions as you first discuss the Business Drivers, and then map your solutions to the client's or prospect's situation.

The diagrams below show the issues your prospect is dealing with and the solutions that you offer. It is important that you understand both the issues and your value.

1.

Business Drivers
- Inventory Turns
- Retail Market Presence
- Flat Earnings
- Changing Distribution Models
- Slow Revenue Growth

2.

Our Capabilities/Resources
- Transaction Pricing Model
- Logistics Experience
- CRM Expertise (Retail)
- Software Integration/Testing
- Off-Shore Programming

You can put all the words you want in the proposal, *but not in the presentation*. And by the way, most proposals are poorly done: too long, boring, and costly to prepare. Other than that, they're great! But, that's a subject for a different book.

Putting It Together

As you can see on the first diagram, Solution Mapping begins with a clear, brief statement of the Business Drivers. Some examples: "Inventory Turns," "Flat Earnings," or "Slow Revenue Growth." These are high-level Business Drivers.

The Business Drivers may be more granular. For example, "Inventory turns are too low," "Competitors sell more per salesperson," or "International distributors are under performing."

The key is to say it in the prospect's words and gain agreement prior to the presentation or discussion, if possible. You want input from your contact and others so that you get it right and don't have to defend your choice of wording. You're not trying to do anything other than to nail the business drivers and get the discussion moving toward possible solutions and potential impact on the business. As you present the Business Drivers, ask for agreement or input. The key is getting it right.

The second diagram, Our Capabilities/Resources, lists the value we can bring to the table. It's not important to list every service, product, or solution we have. It is important to show a reasonable breadth of capability and depth of knowledge. Some will be very important to the prospect; others will be less important. Obviously, if one of our solutions is wildly off the mark don't include it on the chart.

Now the Work Begins

I have to make an assumption . . . you have totally bought into the concept of Intent. In other words, you believe in helping your clients and prospects succeed. Please agree . . . . Excellent! Now we will look at each of the Business Drivers (the problems and opportunities) and ask ourselves how we match up. In the spirit of helping our clients, we may not be the right choice to answer every challenge . . . and that's OK.

If we honestly feel that it's in the prospect's best interest to solve the problem without our help, we should say so. We should even suggest others who can help, assuming we have personal experience with them.

A couple of years ago, I conducted an account planning workshop for a major consulting firm. They wanted to do more business with a large telecommunications company. I asked them to list the challenges their client faced. There were seven the CEO mentioned in the annual report and had discussed in a Wall Street speech. They were tough, challenging issues. The sales team wanted to go after all seven of them. In the spirit of Intent, I asked the group if they truly felt they were the best choice to address *all seven of the issues*. I reminded them that in my opinion, the likelihood of a Fortune 100 company turning these seven key issues over to one outside organization was remote.

Why? Simply too much risk concentration with one organization. It might also show poor judgment on our part to suggest that as outsiders we could solve *all* their problems for them. Assuming we were fortunate enough to present in the boardroom or to an executive carrying our message to the boardroom, we would seem naïve to suggest we could solve all their issues.

At first, the sales team felt I was underselling their capabilities. Nothing could be further from the truth. Cooler heads prevailed, and we selected three to go after. We selected the three based on our credentials and the deep resources needed. We also made the recommendation that we would offer approaches and alternatives to consider for the remaining four issues during the presentation. This was all in the spirit of helping our client. The strategy worked, and my client more than doubled the billings from the prior year with that important client.

The Final Product

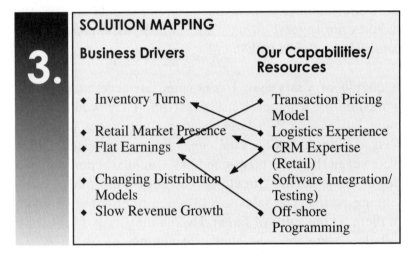

As this final diagram indicates, the Business Drivers are listed in the left-hand column. Then we add our solutions in the right-hand column. Finally, using arrows, we show the linkage between the two. We then discuss the solutions we offer that can meet the challenges.

Would I recommend another company to address one of the issues my company wasn't addressing? Yes, assuming I knew them and their work intimately. It's simply in the best interest of my client to make recommendations based on experience and Insight.

The Referring Physician

The idea of recommending someone else to a client may seem foreign at first. But think about it for a moment. When you go to your family doctor, you may be referred to another doctor, probably a specialist. Do you think poorly of your family doctor for making the suggestion? Not at all. Remember, your primary goal is to get well! You're not there to see if your doctor can do everything in the world of health. So think about the referring physician model when you work with a client and give them your best advice . . . even if it means recommending someone else to help!

SUMMARY

◆ State the customer/prospect Business Drivers in "their" terms and ask for input and agreement—let's work on the right issues!

◆ Map your solutions to the Business Drivers where you are capable of delivering strong and measurable value.

◆ Suggest options and alternatives for Business Drivers outside your scope of services and resources.

◆ Use the Solutions Map to replace many of the Power-Point slides that can make a presentation too long and do not generate good interaction.

TOOL #7: THE QUALIFICATION GRID

When I was working for Accenture, we devised a planning tool for evaluating and prioritizing opportunities with Pfizer, one of the world's major pharmaceutical companies.

It's called the Qualification Grid and you can use it, or a variation of it, to filter your sales pipeline for the best potential business.

Here's how it works: The specific opportunities are listed in the vertical column. You may want to include the key players and the division or department involved. The horizontal columns list the qualifiers—the various factors that affect the quality and viability of the prospective deal.

The qualifiers used in the matrix will naturally vary, but there are some common factors. The following questions will help you chart the grid:

◆ What is the prospect's motivation to buy (increase sales, cut costs, customer service, etc)?

◆ Is government compliance the business driver?

◆ Is the initiative funded and budgeted?

◆ Do we know the decision maker(s)?

◆ Do we have access to them?

◆ When is the decision date/start date?

◆ How will they measure success?

◆ Will this be competitive?

◆ Do we have the resources?

◆ Are we the best choice?

Sample Qualification Grid

Opportunity	Qualifiers										
	Access to decision maker	Internal champion	Project budgeted?	Competitive situation?	Start date	Finish date	Strong ROI?	High priority for buyer?	Can we deliver?	Agreement on results expected?	Request for proposal
Hardware Upgrade	Yes Carol Sutter	Yes Steve Levin	Yes	Yes SCA Inc.	Yes 8/1	No	Yes	Yes	Yes	Yes	Yes
Logistics System (Chicago)	No	Yes Tina Whyte	Yes	??	Q4	??	Yes	??	Yes	??	No
Maintenance Contract	No	Yes Tina Whyte	Yes	??	Q4	??	Yes	??	Yes	No	Yes
Training	Yes Randy Holden	Yes Martha Vines	??	Yes Fast Track, Inc.	Yes 11/1	Yes 3/31	??	No	Partner w/SCS	No	No
1st/2nd Level Help Desk	Yes Chuck Bisesi	Yes Chuck Bisesi	Yes	No	Yes 11/1	N/A	Yes	Yes	Yes	Yes	Yes

I suspect that we all have some form of qualification process. If you worked in a retail store, you'd likely pay close attention to a shopper who expressed the need to make an immediate purchase. I would certainly qualify for that designation the last few shopping days before Christmas! On the other hand, we will need to ask a few qualifying questions of a consumer who is obviously just browsing. Time is important, and we want to invest it wisely.

If you're selling more expensive, and perhaps more complex solutions and products, you must spend more time and effort on the process of qualifying your prospects. The sales cycle may be long and often requires investment in travel, proposal preparation, and company resources to pursue the opportunity.

The Qualification Grid provides a tool for discussion and decision. My experience suggests that weighting each factor may or may not work well, but talking it through with team members or management is extremely helpful and insightful.

Which Questions Are Most Important?

It may sound trite, but all of the questions *can* be significant. It depends on your experience with the prospect. Having said that, I do feel these four are "deal killers," if we come up short:

1.   **What is their motivation to buy?** There must be at least one very compelling problem or opportunity the prospect is trying to address . . . *with* a respected internal champion pounding the table for action.

2.   **Is it funded and budgeted?** Unfunded and unbudgeted projects require major sponsors within the prospect organization and are difficult at best.

3. **How will they measure success?** We must understand their success criteria in deciding if we can meet them. Ultimately, we want to fully understand the metrics they will use in deciding to take action. The answer to this question will also play strongly in creating our business case and value proposition.

4. **Why are we the best choice?** Once we understand the needs of the prospect, we can map our solutions and resources to them. The answer to this question is about strong, specific facts and statements. It's not about glittering generalities, such as "We're committed to customer service," or "We're a global company!" We must have evidence that clearly demonstrates how we will achieve specific results and the positive impact on the prospect's business.

The Qualification Grid is such a useful tool that some organizations have adopted it to determine which sales opportunities will be funded for pursuit and which won't.

Here's the challenge: It is easy to be seduced by an opportunity, particularly if it's one from a highly-visible prospect or customer. You can create a personal mission to "get this deal done," only to waste a lot of time and money chasing something that only had a small chance of success in the first place.

Challenge yourself and your sales team to work through the Qualification Grid on key opportunities. You will improve your chances of winning. It also serves as a great communication tool for anyone who will be working on the opportunity. Modify the Qualification Grid to fit your business, but ask yourself the tough questions that must be answered. This approach will enable you to focus on the best opportunities for the right reasons.

Is Disqualifiying an Oppoturnity a Good Thing?

Have opportunities been disqualified through the use of the grid? Absolutely. The key is to confront positively. In other words, you should have a real concern if you don't know the answer to a question. For example, is the project funded? If you don't know, ask your contact. It's that simple. If you're reluctant to ask, you must determine whether or not this is a serious piece of business . . . both for you and for your prospect!

The voice of experience now speaks. Every salesperson can remember a deal that closed that defied all rules of conduct. It wasn't funded, we didn't have the right contacts, there was an RFP (Request for Proposal), and we didn't know it was being issued, all the signs that scream, "Don't chase this one!" And yet we got the deal. Hey, it happens, but I wouldn't build my business on it. Following a logical process in deciding whether or not to invest your time and the company's resources is just sound business.

Can you follow your heart or your instincts on occasion? You should. But these one-off deals are the exceptions and should be monitored closely. Make your numbers by following processes such as the Qualification Grid first. Then apply whatever remaining time to those "one-off deals" that may happen but seldom do. They are the exception, not the rule.

Consider These Facts

About five years ago I asked some clients how often they won the business when they submitted a proposal. Here's the shocker . . . they hadn't tracked it! I suggested that we try to determine their win rate to see if we could drive it higher.

I followed up on fifty formal proposals with my client. Here are the staggering results: Twenty-one proposals resulted in no action being taken by the prospect!

Since my client was in the outsourcing business, we also found that thirteen of the proposals resulted in internal resources "promising to do a better job," and the idea of outsourcing was squashed.

We also found that their win rate was negligible when they weren't involved early in the RFP process. Conversely, when-ever one of our competitors was involved early, it was amazing how the RFP seemed to favor some of their key strengths and solutions! Early in is a strong competitive tool!

The only really good news was that my client won almost half of the other proposals, and we received some really valuable insight into the whole sales and decision-making process.

My recommendation to the client was to adopt a Qualification Grid and use the grid to examine opportunities, before deciding which ones to really go after. I further suggested that they moni-tor the results quarterly to see if they were disqualifying some opportunities and, most important, to determine if the win rate percentage was moving positively.

Based on that analysis, the win rate did improve. In fact, it almost doubled. We also looked closely at the quality of the proposals they were submitting and made some major changes there as well.

How's This for an Interesting Strategy?

One of the senior partners at a top-tier consulting firm told me about a situation that had "we should pass on this one" written all over it. Their client asked for a proposal on an outsourcing deal. Sounded good until they learned that EDS, the incumbent, had been the provider for almost eight years, through two contract renegotiations.

The senior partner confronted the situation and asked if his firm was being used as a "stalking horse" to get a better deal from the current supplier. His contact acknowledged that they did have a decent relationship with EDS, but "wanted to keep their options open." The positive confrontation at least got the subject on the table. Here's how the dialogue went:

"I'm sure you understand that developing a good proposal takes time and resources. It's expensive and I want to do it for the right reasons," stated the senior partner.

"I understand and look forward to reviewing your proposal," said the prospect.

"Here's my proposition to you. We'll do a thorough job in pulling together a proposal for you. However, we also know that you will probably stick with EDS. Having said that, our proposal will be useful to you in terms of a "second opinion." What I suggest is that we prepare the proposal with the understanding that we have the opportunity to work with you on the supply chain initiative, scheduled for the fourth quarter of this year," countered the senior partner.

"I can't guarantee that you will get *that* work, but I understand your logic and appreciate your willingness to do the proposal on the outsourcing work," responded the prospect.

The senior partner knew enough about the prospect to be willing to invest time and resources in the spirit of building a relationship with a key buyer. By qualifying the opportunity, the senior partner was able to position his firm for future business.

SUMMARY

◆ If you can't answer the questions on your own Qualification Grid, resolve them or take the opportunity out of the sales pipeline.

◆ If you don't have the answers, ask your prospect to help fill in the blanks.

◆ Use the Grid to discuss your sales strategy and to keep everyone informed as you proceed.

◆ Don't get seduced by an opportunity . . . pursue it only if it makes business sense.

◆ Learn to "rule in and rule out" opportunities in order to preserve the precious resources needed to compete for the very best opportunities.

◆ Repeat after me: "We've all won a deal that defied wisdom, but it was the *exception* and *not the rule!*"

TOOL #8: PENETRATE AND RADIATE . . . THE 3X3 MODEL

Think about managing a large, important account. As we discussed, the No. 1 mandate is to "serve well." Being responsive is up there on the list, as well. In addition, one of the highest priorities is developing relationships wide and deep. There's a clear trap in concentrating the majority of your efforts on one or two people. They could very well leave the company, and you may have to start over again.

Another risk in working almost exclusively with one or two people is the limited exposure other key players will have to you, your company, and the kind of work you can deliver. If your day-to-day contact is assigned to another office or placed on a six-month task force, you've got a lot of catching up to do on relationship building. And I'll bet that your competitors know about your current relationships, so they've already begun forging their own relationship with other people in the account.

So let's get proactive and use the approach I call Penetrate and Radiate, the 3X3 Model.

In the typical organization chart, everyone reports to someone and has peers and subordinates. The 3X3 model focuses on the person you have been working with or calling on in the selling process, in this case, Connie Smith. Hopefully, that person will also be one of the key players in making the buying decision.

Organization Chart

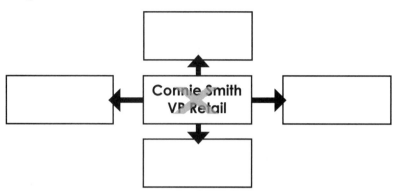

Here's the concept:

Rarely is the final decision to buy made in a vacuum or by only one person. Others in the organization will have to approve the final decision, and still others will influence the decision along the way. Some may challenge the decision or even favor a different supplier. Therefore, by extending your relationships broader and deeper, you can learn about the needs of many people in the organization and also build a potential ground swell of support for your solution.

Extended Organization Chart

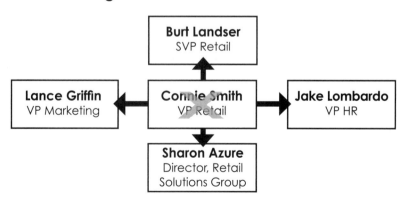

So the model extends as indicated to include other key players above, below, and on the same level as your primary contact. Randall Murphy, founder of Acclivus, a Dallas, Texas, training company, first developed the 3X3 concept.

Penetrate and Radiate: The 3X3 Model in Practice

The approach is based on the realities of the modern organization. Most require that multiple decision makers evaluate and approve a major purchase, particularly one that has enterprise-wide ramifications. To succeed in this environment, we must sell to the broader organization as well.

Most organizations are also in continual flux to one degree or another. By extending our communications to other key players, we reduce the likelihood that a single personnel change, or a single soured relationship, will derail our sales efforts.

Expressed another way, the key players on your 3X3 grid hold considerable influence on the decision. They also have the potential of becoming future sales prospects. Your UniqueConnect to gain access to them is the person you work with on a day-to-day basis and the good work you've done for their company. You may also find other UniqueConnects such as mutual hobbies or an interest in charitable work, but initially it's your day-to-day contact and the work you and your company have performed that are the most influential.

The Power Map

Working the organization now becomes a function of putting together your own "power chart" of the key people and then meeting them as soon as you can. We will begin by determining where our day-to-day contact is on the organization chart and use that as the starting point.

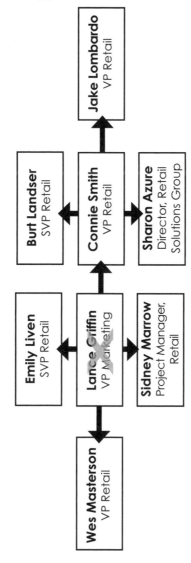

The Power Map Chart

Armed with a diagram of the client organization chart, the discussion sounds something like this:

> "Connie, it would be helpful to me to better understand the organization chart and the reporting structure in which you work. Could you help me fill in the blanks? That way when you or someone else mentions a name or a department, I have a sense of where they fit in and how they might be impacted by our work together."

My personal experience has been very positive concerning my day-to-day contact's willingness to help me understand the organization and the reporting structure. The goal is twofold. First, I just want to get an overview of the names, backgrounds, and responsibilities of the key players. Second, I want to meet them.

So Let's Meet the Boss

Since our primary focus in this book is on growing and retaining key customers, let's begin there. The first order of business is to meet our daily contact's superior, the boss. There may be several approaches, but here are two that have worked for me:

> "Connie, I enjoy working with you. At some point I'd like to meet Burt Landser and say *thank you* for the business we've done together. Could you make the introduction?"
>
> **–OR–**
>
> "Connie, we've made a lot of progress together and I appreciate your support. I would like to *bring my boss,* Stephanie Rollins, in to meet you over the next few weeks. At the same time I wonder if we could introduce her to Burt Landser, as well."

These are both legitimate requests based on a good working relationship and mutual trust. You should score at least 80 percent using these techniques. You will also gain access to Burt Landser's office when and if we need it in the future. You'll learn more about the company and watch how Connie and her boss interact. Valuable Information and Insight.

Here's another idea that could have value. You might ask Connie if there is anything you or your boss can mention during the visit with Burt Landser that would help her or her department. Sometimes an outside voice can introduce an idea with the decision maker that's very helpful to your daily contact. For example, a comment concerning how well Connie's team has worked with your team can add value and will be appreciated. Just make sure it's a sincere comment and not construed by anyone as fluff.

Time to Meet Some of Connie's Peer Group

Our confidence is up. We've met with Connie's boss and we're beginning to get the idea of working an organization. Next stop is the peer group.

Undoubtedly, when you make a sale, other managers and departments in the organization will be affected. Imagine the impact on other departments when new software is installed in the finance department. In another example, the decision to open a second distribution center will require that other departments get involved, logistics or manufacturing, for example.

Meeting members of management at the same level as your daily contact broadens your understanding of the interaction going on daily. It's courteous to let other decision makers know such things as anticipated delivery schedules or training dates for their planning purposes. Answering questions and providing information will help the other managers do a better job. In addition, they may well influence present and future decisions. And who knows? Handled professionally, there just might be a chance to work on some of their problems and opportunities in the future!

Here's the direct path I take to meet the peer group:

> "Connie, I looked at the organization chart and it appears that at least two other departments will be impacted by this decision: Marketing and Human Resources. How can we set up a meeting with them to **brief them** and **answer any questions** they may have? My experience is that they will appreciate the heads up and may have some good suggestions for us."

Once again, there is no hidden agenda. You have to believe that the more you know about an organization and its people, the better you can help them be successful. Connie's peer group didn't get to their positions without working hard and smart. Getting them involved is the right thing to do.

Let's Hear It for the Legal Department!

We were trying very hard to sell a multimillion dollar inventory management system to a large manufacturer. It was competitive, but we felt we were in a decent position to win. As we met more of the prospect's management team, it became clear that the decision would be made by consensus. Based on that, we tried to meet all the executives we could.

We eventually won the contract and debriefed the win with them, so we could learn more about the whole process. The president talked about our willingness to listen to them. He added, "I asked each of my direct reports for their feedback on your company. When I asked our legal counsel, he said that you had brought over the contracts you typically use and also the names of your legal staff and outside legal counsel. He felt that information would save time in the negotiating process." By understanding the idea of meeting peers as well as subordinates and superiors, we were building a consensus. And we thought lawyers were bad people!

Finding the "Rising Stars"

Most organizations have succession plans in place. They provide for an orderly progression of people into jobs with more responsibility. The plan involves identifying the talented future leaders, preparing them for more responsibility, and keeping the business moving forward. As an aside, it also helps in retaining the best people because they know they have been identified as "high potential." Most organizations groom talent in this manner or through a similar process.

Extended Organization Chart

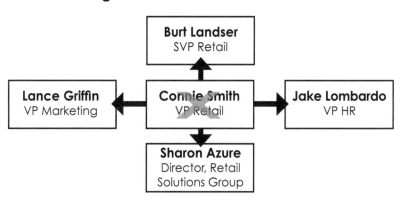

So let's get back to our 3X3 Model and meet some of Connie's direct reports. We want to meet them for several reasons. First, they may be selected to help with our project. Second, they will have Insight into the organization. Third, some of their thoughts and perhaps concerns will reflect the thinking of others at that level. We want to hear the feedback early in the selling or install-ing phases so we can take corrective action.

A Narrow Miss

We were getting ready to install a new bank teller system for a large regional banking customer. Our client loved the speed and flexibility of the system and wanted it installed over a three-day weekend, Labor Day to be specific. Systems are often installed that way in order to take advantage of an additional day for test-ing and dealing with any immediate problems.

Following the principle of meeting other people in the bank by using the 3X3 model, we interviewed the head teller and two members of his staff in the spirit of sharing information. Boy, did we get an earful! He brought up two examples of poor installations that "almost shut down the bank."

His suggestion was to begin training the front line people imme-diately, pay overtime if necessary, and avoid confusion on the first day back to work. That's exactly what we then suggested, and it was approved. We agreed with the head teller when he said that you can't put your front line people at risk and disap-point the customer because of their inability to understand the new system.

So it's time to ask Connie to introduce us to some direct reports, hopefully "rising stars." We've targeted Sharon Azure, Director of the Retail Solutions Group. Here's how it goes:

> "Connie, I know that you will be looking at several of your staff to be very involved with the project. As you begin the selection process, I would really like to meet the candidates. That way, I will have some rapport with them before we get down to the hard work. I can also give you

some feedback, if it would help you. When would it be possible to meet people, such as Sharon Azure?"

Once again, nothing tricky, no sleight of hand. It's just the whole idea of knowing the organization and its people so you can do a better job.

What Should We Expect of Ourselves?

Here's the minimum goal for 3X3: You want to meet at least one person who outranks your contact, preferably, his or her manager. Then you want introductions to at least two peers and two subordinates.

As you meet these people, you've got two tasks to keep 3X3 alive and meaningful. First, update the organization chart with the names and enter the new information gained into your CRM system, electronic or manual. Second, use each new contact to begin a new 3X3 with him or her as the center point, as indicated on the "The Power Map."

The Power Map Chart

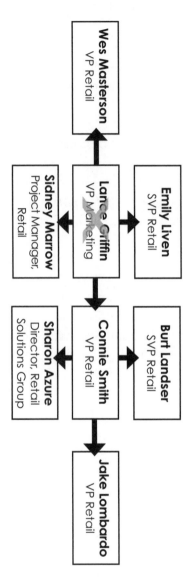

	Wes Masterson VP Retail	
Sidney Marrow Project Manager, Retail	**Lance Griffin** VP Marketing	**Emily Liven** SVP Retail
Sharon Azure Director, Retail Solutions Group	**Connie Smith** VP Retail	**Burt Landser** SVP Retail
	Jake Lombardo VP Retail	

Use the 3X3 tool effectively and your customers may pay you a handsome compliment. They'll introduce you by saying, "I want you to meet someone who probably knows as much about our company as we do!"

SUMMARY

♦ When two or more products or services appear to be similar in benefits and cost, people tend to buy based on relationships . . . not always, but it is highly likely.

♦ The Penetrate and Radiate (or 3X3) concept provides a map of key players, a logical plan to follow, and creates the basis for expanded relationships at multiple levels of the organization.

♦ We're vulnerable if we lock ourselves in to just one person. If that person leaves, gets promoted, or changes responsibilities we have to start over.

♦ Set an annual goal of revising and expanding your 3X3 by at least five new contacts.

♦ If you work with a team of people, challenge them to "3X3 the customer" and then share the Insight gained.

TOOL #9: THE RELATIONSHIP MAP

This tool will help you build a visual picture of your Relation-ship Plan and activities. It's excellent for keeping a presence with your key contacts, budgeting your time and investment, and establishing Mind Share. By following the Relationship Map, you are wagering that the better the relationship, the greater the Mind Share. My experience and that of many others indicates it's a wager you'll collect!

The guiding principle is that when a product or service is equal to or close to being equal that of a competitor, people will over-whelmingly buy based on the best relationship.

"But We Already Use a Customer Relationship Man-agement System."

There are many good systems available for managing client and prospect information. These systems allow the user to capture the names, titles, and contact information of decision makers. Then additional information about both past activities and future plans for each identified person can be added.

The Relationship Map leverages any Customer Relationship Management (CRM) system by establishing a consistent, planned series of touch points with your clients. Some CRM systems will let you enter the Relationship Map into the database. If so, do it. The important thing is that you think about the key people, the frequency, and the type of contact you want to have. By combin-ing the best of CRM with the Relationship Map, you position yourself as a business partner who values good relationships. In turn, you will be keeping yourself and your company "top of mind" when there is an opportunity for your services. **Mind Share drives Market Share!**

How Does It Work?

You can do a Relationship Map for several companies or for just one, depending on the size and complexity of the organizations. The first step is to list your key contacts down the left hand column. You'll have all the contact information in your database, so just the name and title is all you need now. You will have to be the judge on how many people to list in the contact column. This will be based on the sales potential with the company, the time you can devote, and the budget constraints.

Once you've listed the contact names, enter the relationship activities across the top. You'll notice from the sample Relationship Map that I've included several to consider. This is where Information and Insight are so important. You can tailor the Relationship Map by applying your knowledge of the account and the individual to have maximum impact.

Sample Relationship Map

Company	Name & Title	Relationship Activities							
		Executive Call	Deliver Article	Client Breakfast Briefing	Sports Event	Social Event	Open House	Client Tour	Industry Conf.
The Hopkins Co.	Mark Hopkins SVP	8/23	9/15	10/25		Theatre 12/1			IPA 3/15
	Susan Bucher VP	8/23	9/15	10/25		Musical 12/15			IPA 3/15
	Mike Twain VP	8/23	9/15	10/25	Golf 11/12				IPA 3/15
Palmer-Johnson	Luis Alstott Partner	8/23		4/1	Hockey 5/15		8/1	6/18	
	Henry Lechner Partner	8/23		4/1	Hockey 5/15		8/1	6/18	
	Sarah Church Manager	8/23		4/1			8/1	6/18	

Which Activity Is Best?

What works best? My experience has been that interesting, even provocative information is high on the list. Therefore, White Papers, published articles, pertinent research reports, and Points of View usually get favorable reviews.

A **White Paper** is the title applied to a body of information representing your organization's best thinking on a specific subject. The White Paper is usually published by the company and written by one or more of its employees. It's designed to show thought leadership and critical thinking. Examples of a White Paper might be on the subject of security on the Internet or future applications of wireless technology. The White Paper is not a sales brochure! It is the best thinking your organization has on an important topic and should have an academic look and feel to it.

A **Point of View (POV),** on the other hand, is applying some of the organization's best thinking on information provided by a third party. For example, an article appears in an industry publication. After reviewing the article, your company feels strongly—has a Point of View about the content in the article. The POV may be wildly supportive or may take issue with the article and attempt to show another side to the issue at hand. A POV is not intended to merely agree or disagree with the article. It must take a stand and present facts, metrics, case studies, or research to substantiate its position on the article or publication.

You can also have a POV on current trends or even on commonly-accepted statements or subjects. For example, it has been very fashionable to publicly state how important having offshore programming capability is to the user or provider of technology.

This commonly-accepted statement may be the subject of a POV that points out the need for appropriate security, understanding of the cross-cultural implications of an American-based company using offshore resources, and tight quality management. Your POV may be that "cheaper" is one criterion, but there are others that must be considered as well.

What Else Works?

In addition to Information, what works in building relationships? In no certain order, here are several to consider:

◆ Events
◆ Conferences
◆ Briefings over lunch or breakfast
◆ Tours of interesting facilities or installations
◆ Social activities

Bringing in an outside speaker to conduct a workshop or make a keynote address can be very effective. There are two approaches to consider: having the event for several clients and prospects, or hosting it just for the decision makers of one organization. In the latter event, you will get more open and honest interplay with the speaker or workshop facilitator, if that's the goal.

I learned the hard way that not all executives like early breakfast briefings or off-site lunches. We planned an 8:00 a.m. breakfast briefing with an outside speaker for clients and prospects in New York City. Sounded good until we realized that the majority of our attendees commuted, many by train. We had poor attendance and shifted to luncheon briefings! Make certain that you understand the logistics and culture of both the city and the companies you consider. A speaker over breakfast, lunch, or dinner? Do your homework before quickly selecting **your own favorite venue!** You certainly don't want to have a speaker during lunch or dinner in Paris, France! Dining is the main agenda, and the speaker will be viewed as a distasteful interruption.

The process of matching activities to each person is important and requires an understanding of his or her interests. For example, attending the theater may appeal to one person while another may be more interested in a round of golf. In some cases, your key player may totally separate business from social activities and be interested only in critical information from seminars and workshops.

How Often Should We Engage?

The answer to this question is . . . just enough to have a polite presence and maintain Mind Share. You can clearly overdo it, so ask your prospects and clients. I've found that they can be remarkably honest about the frequency and type of relationship building that they value and enjoy.

A large commercial real estate firm encourages their senior brokers to "Touch Twelve." The program provides information and events the broker can choose from in order to "touch" each key client once a month. Based on several years of evaluation, the program works well for them. So it really depends on budget, resources, and the client's input.

Personally, I've had great success with a quarterly approach to the Relationship Map. My poorest results came from cramming too many activities and information into a short time frame. For example, multiple events scheduled at the beginning of the year or around budget-setting time may not work. People are very busy then, and your event may not make the "must do" list.

A Couple of Good Lessons

Avoid the big bang theory of relationship planning. This occurs when we bet most of our budget on one big event for the year. The foundation of Integrated Marketing, an approach many attribute to Northwestern University, is a consistent set of marketing messages, relationship activities, and information exchange spaced over a year or more. This concept of Key Messages delivered in a variety of formats is a prime component of building an effective Relationship Map.

Once the Relationship Map is built and executed, follow-up by the sales team will provide feedback on effectiveness from both their individual perception and more importantly, from the clients and prospects. Updates and modifications can then be made to keep the Map fresh and relevant. There is nothing wrong with a big event, but my experience is that you need more than just one event to have lasting impact. The best of both worlds might be a big event linked with quarterly events held locally. Budget permitting, of course!

Off to the Links!

Your boss likes golf, so golf it is. That may make many of us happy, but there are prospects and clients who simply don't like golf. There are also some who would rather have an evening at home instead of joining you at the theater. Planning events or activities because *we* like them is not rational. You may guess correctly, but why not have several different venues from which to choose? Many organizations have found that including the prospect's or client's "significant other" increases attendance, particularly at a social function. Busy decision makers work long hours, many of them on the road; therefore, being able to include their significant other makes your event less intrusive into scarce personal time.

A High-Return Example

Earlier we stated that prospects and clients always appreciate good information. True. I've also found that *provocative information* based on research or just plain enlightened thinking can find the mark with people.

About five years ago, my client did an in-depth study of retail banking and found that many of the industry's commonly accepted "facts" about retail banking customers were wrong. So the program, called "The Seven Myths of Retail Banking," began with a mailing and concluded with a series of breakfast briefings to share the research. The effort met with enthusiastic response from the attendees and helped my client further position themselves as "true thought leaders." By combining good research, a strong POV, and a forum for discussion; my client leveraged multiple facets of good Integrated Marketing.

Put your Relationship Map in place, monitor it closely, and stay the course!

SUMMARY

◆ A Relationship Map can be as valuable in selling as a Work Plan is for a new project.

◆ Spread varied activities over the year and mix business and social events. Not everyone wants just golf, or just theater, or just breakfast briefings.

◆ Ask for feedback from customers and prospects on your activities and adjust accordingly.

◆ Make the Relationship Map an integral part of your CRM and Sales Force Automation programs.

◆ Leverage events. For example, at a social function, take pictures and produce an album for delivery afterwards.

◆ Another leverage idea is to summarize a guest speaker's remarks and distribute them after the speech to both the attendees and those who couldn't attend . . . it will demonstrate what they missed if they weren't there!

TOOL # 10: THE WIN/LOSS REVIEW

The game is over, the teams have showered and left the locker room, and the fans are driving home. Not long after the noise has died down, the coaching staff will look at films of the game and begin to critique the team's performance.

What worked and what didn't? Why? What changes will we need for next week's contest?

The golf pro tells you to make minor adjustments on the next swing. You try and he tapes it. "Let's try it again," he encourages. After the session, you both watch the videotape to see how you've done during the lesson. Some things have improved and others need additional attention. Now it's back to the practice range to continue improving your game.

In a training class conducted for new product training, or perhaps customer service training, the instructor makes assignments and provides coaching and feedback for the attendees as they tackle the issue at hand. If the feedback is positive, everyone can build on the success. If improvement is required, additional time will be spent refining the areas needing attention.

Whether on the football field, the golf course, in a classroom, or at an office selling a product, improvement comes much quicker with review and feedback.

Let's Look at Some Film!

At some point, you either get the sale or you don't. The deal closes or it doesn't. There's ink on the contract or the pen is still in your pocket.

If you get the win, it's time to celebrate . . . and then to get down to work for your new client. If you're on the losing side of the decision, it's on to the next prospect. But before we close the books, whether we've won or lost, there is one final and important step in the sales process.

That's the Win/Loss Review. It's a structured analysis of what went right and what went wrong during the pursuit of the sale. It's a chance to sit down with your prospect or client to better understand how and why the decision was made. In other words, what **really** went on during the process of making the final choice?

A well-formulated Win/Loss Review should be seen as a learning tool, and as a way to improve your sales planning and overall execution. It should not be used as a means to punish or eliminate salespeople.

Instead, use this opportunity to gain Insight into what occurred on the "other side of the desk." By asking direct questions and listening closely to the responses, you are then in a position to improve future selling efforts by using the Information you've gathered.

Planning the Review

Here are a couple of guidelines that can help you plan a successful Win/Loss Review.

First, the person who was most closely involved in trying to sell the business **should not** conduct the review. That person is simply too close to the situation and cannot be expected to render an objective assessment of the outcome. Nor can a prospect be expected to provide totally honest feedback to the salesperson who did not win the deal. It's just too difficult for most people to deliver more bad news to someone who worked hard but did not win the business. This is compounded if the sales person's boss goes on the debriefing. Very few prospects want to get someone in trouble.

We want the unvarnished truth. So in most cases, it's best to have someone from your company, an outside third party, or a consultant plan and conduct the Win/Loss Review. They bring a fresh perspective to the evaluation. Especially in Loss Reviews, prospects may be more willing to divulge difficult or critical assessments to a third party.

Most prospect companies are willing to sit down for a post-decision evaluation. Many firms conduct these Win-Loss debriefings of their own sales performances. The overall idea is to learn and improve, not find fault and blame.

If possible, try to meet with the person who worked the deal most closely from the prospect side. Ask to speak to others who may have influenced the decision, such as staff-level personnel, peers, and superiors. You can use the 3X3 grid introduced earlier in the Tools Section as a guide to who might be included in the Win/Loss discussions.

The Key Questions

For most reviews, you should concentrate on eight to ten questions, and be prepared to ask follow-up questions as appropriate. Write the questions down ahead of time, and seek the input of the salespeople involved when formulating the questions.

It may help to submit your questions to the individuals being interviewed prior to the meeting so they can prepare for the session and talk to others in the company to get their thoughts. In addition, it shows respect by efficiently using their time.

Of course, wins and losses are dramatically different animals, and you should plan your questions accordingly. First let's look at some of the questions following a loss.

We Lost, Now Let's Learn

Defeat, they say, builds character. At the very least, we should use any lost deal as an opportunity to turn ourselves into better salespeople.

A well-done Loss Review can tell you a lot about both your prospect and yourself. When requesting a review, make it clear to your former prospects that you consider this a learning opportunity. Ask them to be straightforward and direct, so that you can learn from the experience. Assure them that the information will be used with discretion, and emphasize that the review is *not an attempt* to reopen the sales process.

Here are some of the questions that might be raised in a typical Loss Review.

◆ What was the process used in making the final decision?

◆ When was the decision made?

◆ What were the key differences between the winner and those who didn't win?

◆ What did the prospect feel were our strengths?

◆ What did the prospect feel were our weaknesses?

◆ Besides price, what key factors influenced the decision?

◆ If the prices were identical, would we have won?

◆ How could our proposal and presentation have been improved?

◆ Did we make any debilitating mistakes?

◆   What can we do to keep the door open for future opportunities?

I cannot emphasize enough that Loss Reviews should be conducted in a positive and highly professional manner. Don't whine or complain. Thank them for their input. Make a graceful exit.

What About Frank?

A couple of years ago I did a Loss Review on a very competitive computer operations outsourcing opportunity. The client was a large Fort Worth, Texas, retailer and the stakes were high: a multiple-year, multimillion dollar contract. Several weeks following the delivery of the final proposal, our sales team was informed that a competitor had been selected, and I was asked to do the Loss Review.

During interviews with the Chief Information Officer (CIO) and other members of the management team, I asked if we had neglected to ask any pertinent questions during our sales initiatives. The CIO said, "Yes, and it concerned the president of the company. He was one of the first to get a personal computer and did it to show his commitment to our new technology initiatives."

He went on to tell me that the president regularly called a long-time employee named Frank for help with his computer. Frank had built a special rapport during years of working directly with the president.

"Our president expressed concern that by outsourcing computer operations, he would lose his personal 'help desk' in the person of Frank! Your competitor had discussed this special need for executive assistance during their sales efforts, and you didn't," he finished.

Would we have won the deal if we had known about Frank? Who knows? However, it helped point out the need to ask each and every question when you are making major changes in the way a prospect will be doing business, based on your products and solutions. I sometimes wonder how Frank is doing . . .

A Word of Caution

Above all, **do not** use the Loss Review as a chance to resell the account. If you ask for a review and then try to reopen the decision, your prospect will resent it, and rightly so. Word will get around, and soon nobody will be willing to sit down for a feedback session.

In my experience, it's extraordinarily rare for a company to reopen an opportunity once a decision has been made. In the rare instance that a company does revisit a decision, let them bring it up in the natural conduct of the Win/Loss Review. Again, in my experience, I have never seen a decision reversed during a Win/Loss Review.

Use your Loss Review as a unique opportunity to learn from your mistakes . . . not to make another one!

Hoist the Flag, We've Won; Now Let's Find Out Why!

One very common error I see in the world of sales is the failure to debrief a Win.

I suppose that's understandable. The emotions are high and everyone is celebrating. Some sales offices bang gongs, throw a few down at the local watering hole, and talk about how good it's going to be! This is a time when salespeople pump their fists in the air and start daydreaming about how to spend that bonus. Enjoy yourself a bit. You've earned it!

But now is also a perfect time to evaluate exactly how and why you won the day.

People who have not experienced the ups and downs of direct selling may think it was a winning smile and smooth manner that sealed the deal. That classic stereotype of sales professionals couldn't be further from the truth. In most big-ticket wins, it takes a lot more than that! So right now, while people are energized and memories are fresh, we should sit down and analyze exactly how we landed the business.

The Timing's Perfect

The majority of clients are very willing to take part in a Win Review. You and your company have been chosen; you are viewed as business partners or at least good people with whom to do business. The client is more relaxed because it's a positive environment, not an unpleasant one.

As with the Loss Review, we hope to gain Insight into how and why the decision was made, and then to use that information to polish and improve our future sales performance. Common Win Review questions will include some of the same ones used in the Loss Review, such as how the final decision was made, how important price was, the process they went through, and so forth. Additional questions should be considered in conducting a Win Review. For example:

◆ What did our competitors do that impressed you?

◆ Who had the best proposal and/or presentation? What stood out about the proposal or presentation?

◆ Who showed the most creativity in their final solution and proposal?

◆ What were our competitor's strengths and weaknesses?

◆ If the timing of the decision differed from expectations, why?

◆ How effective was our follow-up?

◆ What were the key factors (quality of solution, relationship, price, other) in the decision?

◆ Was there a significant internal debate over the decision?

◆ Are there any people we should talk to or meet based on our winning the business? (This gives your client an opportunity to "mend fences" if someone favored another company and not yours.)

In some ways, a Win Review can be even more productive than a Loss Review. After a Win, you can learn things that help you improve your sales performance and competitive positioning going forward. Your new customer might naturally be open to sharing information about your competitors, and perhaps providing you with early "storm warnings" that a competitor is really on the move and should be monitored closely in the future.

As a general guideline, I like to know who came in second and what was most impressive about their efforts. I can learn from my competition, and it's particularly helpful to hear it from a client who just went through the buying process.

A Win Review can also be viewed as a natural doorway to the process of managing the customer relationship. Listen carefully to both the positives and negatives, and then adjust both the sales and production sides of your business accordingly.

Applying the Lessons Learned

During a Win Review with a West Coast drugstore chain, we were complimented on our thoroughness, attention to detail, and solid transition plan to the new system. While the sales team felt good in hearing the feedback, we were even more interested when our client said, "Your primary competitor did a really good job of bringing in relevant work examples they had from outside the drugstore industry. Our senior management felt they shed a new perspective on a couple of areas of the business."

You can bet that we included the notion of sharing Best Practices from two perspectives following that valuable Insight from our client. First, we included Best Practices from our direct industry work. Second, we added examples of high-value work from outside the client's immediate industry. Smart businesspeople can "connect the dots" when presented with stimulating and fresh thinking, whether it's directly in their industry or not.

Learn from your wins and you'll have a lot more of them.

SUMMARY

- ◆ Use an objective party, not the salesperson, to debrief in a Win/Loss Review.

- ◆ Avoid the temptation to re-open the sale in a review — it's just not professional or fair!

- ◆ Conduct reviews for both Wins and Losses — it's a valuable learning experience.

- ◆ Share the Insight from a review with the management and sales teams.

- ◆ Be willing to use the new information to modify your "go-to market strategy" if it's not effective.

CONCLUSION

Selling in the boardroom is a noble goal. However, few of us actually make a presentation, let alone a sales call, to a board of directors. It generally doesn't happen that way. But the message is this: if you have the opportunity to present to a board of directors, you will give that mission total focus and energy.

What would you do differently if you were given the chance to sell in the boardroom? Certainly you'd do lots of homework on both the company and its directors. You'd know the history of the company, the directors' backgrounds, recent performance of the company, and competitors; the list goes on and on. Why would you take the time to do all this preparation? **Simple.**

You've got one chance to make a favorable impression and you want to be at your best. So doesn't it make sense to adopt that same mindset on every call we make?

A sales call doesn't have to be in the boardroom to be important. It might be a follow-up call with someone you met at a trade show or at an industry function. It could be as basic as an insurance agent talking to a young couple about their first insurance policy in their "boardroom"—the table in their kitchen! The point is your sales success will increase by combining the concepts of Intent, Information, Insight, UniqueConnect, and the proven Tools we covered in the second half of the book.

William Shakespeare once wrote, "Brevity is the soul of wit." Following that advice, here is a brief summary to show you how to put "teeth" into the concepts covered in Boardroom Selling.

◆ Avoid cold calls like the plague ... Find a UniqueConnect for every call.

◆ You can double your business by concentrating on current customers and references from them.

◆ Even if you and your company are not the right fit for the prospect today, your Intent is to help make their business successful. They'll be back at the right time, and more importantly, they will perceive you as a true professional.

◆ Construct your Key Messages with Proof Points—validation that what you're saying has merit and measurable value.

◆ A clear follow-up plan after sales calls is essential, but it shouldn't be one-sided. It's irritating to constantly ask if they've made a decision or if they need any more information. Follow-up calls should bring new ideas or simply say, "I just wanted to check in to see how you were doing."

◆   Be enthusiastic about the value that you and your company can provide. If you're not excited, why would the prospect care?

◆   Learn to ask the question, **"How can I earn the right to do business with you?"** The emphasis is on the word **"earn."**

A final thought. Selling is a very competitive occupation. You are competing not only with your competitors, but also for time, attention, and budget. These don't come easily to most decision makers. By applying the principles in this book, you will mark yourself as a professional with something valuable to say.